Betty Crocker's

New Low-Fat, Low-Cholesterol

Cookbook

MACMILLAN • USA

MACMILLAN

A Simon & Schuster Macmillan Company
1633 Broadway
New York, NY 10019-6785

Library of Congress Cataloging-in-Publication Data

Crocker, Betty
Betty Crocker's new low-fat, low-cholesterol cookbook.

p. cm.

Rev. ed. of : Betty Crocker's low-fat, low cholesterol cookbook, 1991.

Includes index.
ISBN: 0-02-860388-5: (alk. paper)

1. Low-fat diet diet—Recipes. 2. Low-cholesterol diet—Recipes.

I. Crocker, Betty. Betty Crocker's low-fat, low-cholesterol cookbook. II. Title.

RM237.7.C75	1996
641.5'638—dc20	95-16653
	CIP

GENERAL MILLS, INC.

Betty Crocker Food and Publications Center

Director: Marcia Copeland
Editor: Karen Coune
Recipe Development: Mary Carroll, Mary E. Peterson, Julie H. Turnbull
Food Stylists: Kate Courtney Condon, Cindy Lund, Mary Hallin Johnson

Nutrition Department
Nutritionists: Elyse A. Cohen, M.S., Nancy Holmes, R.D.

Photographic Services
Photographer: Carolyn Luxmore

Cover by Iris Jeromnimon
Designed by Michele Laseau/George J. McKeon

For consistent baking results, the Betty Crocker Food and
Publications Center recommends Gold Medal flour.

Manufactured in the United States of America
10 9 8 7 6 5 4 3 2 1
First edition

Cover: Seafood Stew with Rosamarina (page 104),
Back cover: Chocolate Swirl Cheesecake with Raspberry Topping (page 185)
Frontis: Three-Pepper Stir-fry (page 170)
Contents: 1. An abundance of delicious, nutritious low-fat foods (page 6); 2. Green Herb Dip (page 30);
3. Gingered Flank Steak (page 50); 4. Chicken Breasts with Sun-dried Tomato Sauce (page 76);
5. Szechuan Vegetables with Rice (page 138); 6. Warm Greens with Balsamic Vinnigrette (page 175);
7. Three-Berry Sorbet (page 200) and Biscotti (page 204)

Introduction

You don't have to be falling apart to think seriously about healthy eating. Health is one of the biggest news items in America today. Reports in medical journals indicating foods that can lower cholesterol levels make TV headlines. But different studies turn up contradictory evidence, leaving you to wonder, "What does it mean for me?"

We first answered that question with *Betty Crocker's Low-Fat, Low-Cholesterol Cookbook*. A total guide to healthful eating and cooking, it offered recipes for delicious low-fat, low-cholesterol dishes plus all the information you needed to make your own choices for a healthy diet. In the meantime, however, government and Congress have legislated new labeling and developed the Food Guide Pyramid, to name a few changes.

That's where *Betty Crocker's New Low-Fat, Low-Cholesterol Cookbook* comes in. This new edition of the Betty Crocker best-seller brings you up to date on the latest thinking and makes sense of the Nutrition Facts labels, the Food Guide Pyramid and government definitions of such terms as "light" and "low fat." Our low-fat, low-cholesterol dishes are as satisfying as in the first edition, and many draw on the newly available fat-free/cholesterol-free and low-fat/low-cholesterol ingredients. Plus, we've added symbols for low fat, moderate fat, low cholesterol and moderate cholesterol, so you can find the recipes you want quickly.

As in the first edition, each recipe provides complete nutrition information per serving. There are recipe makeovers that show you how to cut the fat in you own recipes along with tips for low-fat cooking. Those looking for help with meal planning will find low-fat menus for every occasion. You can even figure out how many of your daily calories are fat calories; just follow the steps explained on page 23.

For low-fat, high-flavor ideas, flip through the more than 175 recipes and 45 full-color photos in *Betty Crocker's New Low-Fat, Low-Cholesterol Cookbook*. It just might change the way you eat.

Betty Crocker

ontents

Nutrition Symbols

Every one of the delicious recipes in this book meets at least one of the five nutritional criteria shown below, many meet several. See page 27 for more details.

LOW CALORIE

LOW FAT

MODERATE FAT

LOW CHOLESTEROL

MODERATE CHOLESTEROL

1

Here's to Your Health

- Use nonstick cookware and nonstick cooking spray to decrease the amount of oil needed in cooking.

- Cook onions, garlic or chopped vegetables in water, broth, apple juice, flavored vinegars or wine instead of oil, butter or margarine.

- Choose low-fat or fat-free versions of dairy products.

- Choose herbs, spices, mustard, lemon juice or flavored vinegars instead of butter or oils to boost the flavor of plain foods.

- Cut the amount of fat or oil in a regular recipe by one-fourth. If that yields good results, keep reducing the fat until you find the minimum that will still produce an appealing dish.

An abundance of delicious, nutritious low-fat foods.

Here's to Your Health

Good health, a long life, happiness—these are goals many of us share. A healthful lifestyle can help us reach these goals, and although there may be individual variations, there are some common themes.

Healthful eating and exercise habits are extremely important in the pursuit of a healthful lifestyle. In the following pages, we'll explore just what healthful eating is all about and look briefly at the importance of regular exercise. You may be surprised to learn that pleasure can be part of a healthful lifestyle and, in fact, is vital to it!

Cutting Down on Fat and Cholesterol

One overriding dietary concern today is the amount of fat we eat. High blood cholesterol is a major risk factor for coronary heart disease

Risk Factors for Coronary Heart Disease

High blood cholesterol	Vascular disease
High blood pressure	Obesity
Family history of coronary heart disease before the age of 55	Being male
Cigarette smoking	Sedentary lifestyle
Diabetes	

Total Serum Cholesterol Classification

Desirable Serum Cholesterol	**Borderline-high Serum Cholesterol**	**High Serum Cholesterol**
Below 200 mg/dl	200–239 mg/dl	240 mg/dl and above

LDL Cholesterol Classification

Desirable	**Borderline-high Risk**	**High Risk**
Less than 130 mg/dl	130–150 mg/dl	160 mg/dl and above

HDL Cholesterol Classification

Desirable
Above 35 mg/dl

Source: Report of the Expert Panel on Detection, Evaluation and Treatment of High Blood Cholesterol in Adults, *National Cholesterol Education Program, National Heart, Lung and Blood Institute, U.S. Dept. of Health and Human Services, NIH Publication 88-2926, 1987.*

(CHD), our nation's number one killer. And more than any other dietary factor, saturated fat in the diet can raise our blood cholesterol levels. Less fat, however, means fewer calories—an extra incentive to keep our fat intake down.

According to the National Institutes of Health (NIH), more than 50 percent of all adult Americans have blood cholesterol levels higher than "desirable." Half of these people have levels that are considered "high."

Currently, almost 38 percent of the calories in the average American diet comes from fat. This represents about 84 grams of total fat in a typical 2,000-calorie diet. Eighty-four grams of fat would be, for example, about 7 1/2 tablespoons or almost 1/2 cup of solid margarine per day. The American Heart Association (AHA) and many other health organizations recommend that healthy adults reduce their total fat intake to less than 30 percent of daily calories (about 65 grams in a 2,000-calorie diet); that's easy to calculate, as you can see on page 23.

In addition to the problem of high fat intake, our dietary cholesterol levels are higher than they should be. Average cholesterol intakes now stand at 350 to 400 milligrams daily. Health experts suggest we limit daily intake to less than 300 milligrams of cholesterol.

What many of us don't realize, however, is that we need some fat. You may be interested to know that fat and cholesterol play very positive roles in good health.

What Is Fat?

Over the past forty years, we've cut down on our intake of fat from animal sources. Today we're eating more vegetable fats in the form of salad dressings and oils. The greatest amount of fat in the average American diet, however, still comes from meat, fish and poultry. Looking at the pie

chart below you can see how fat contributes to our daily diets.

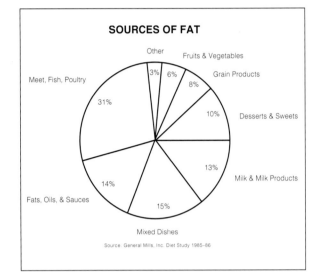

SOURCES OF FAT

- Other 3%
- Fruits & Vegetables 6%
- Grain Products 8%
- Meet, Fish, Poultry 31%
- Desserts & Sweets 10%
- Milk & Milk Products 13%
- Mixed Dishes 15%
- Fats, Oils, & Sauces 14%

Source: General Mills, Inc. Diet Study 1985–86

Fat helps keep us healthy, though, in several ways because it:

- Provides linoleic acid, a fatty acid essential to proper growth, healthy skin and metabolism of cholesterol.

- Helps transport, absorb and store the fat-soluble vitamins A, D, E and K.

- Insulates and cushions body organs.

- Supplies energy. It's the most concentrated source of calories (nine calories per gram of fat versus four calories per gram for protein and carbohydrate).

- Satisfies us. Because it takes longer to digest, fat stays with us longer, helping to control hunger. What's more, it tastes good!

Fats are made up of carbon, hydrogen and oxygen atoms. Different kinds of fats are distinguished by differences in their chemical structure. The building blocks of fat are fatty acids. Fatty acids are saturated, monounsaturated or polyunsaturated.

Saturated Versus Unsaturated Fats

Saturated fats are solid at room temperature and are found mainly in animal sources. Foods that contain higher amounts of saturated fats include meats, eggs and dairy products (whole milk, hard cheese, butter and cream). Tropical fats—coconut, palm and palm kernel oils—are unique because they come from plants, yet they, too, contain significant amounts of saturated fat.

Scientific evidence demonstrates a link between a diet high in saturated fats and the incidence of high blood cholesterol. All saturated fats, however, do not have the same cholesterol-raising potential. (Research conducted using palm oil, which is high in saturated fatty acids, indicates that it behaves differently from other saturated fats. Why these differences exist is not clear, and more research is needed to study the long-term effects of these fatty acids on blood cholesterol levels.)

Fats and oils that contain mainly unsaturated fatty acids are liquid at room temperature and are found most commonly in plant sources. Substituting these fats for saturated fats may help to lower blood cholesterol levels. Olive oil and peanut oil are high in *mono*unsaturated fats, while corn, soybean, safflower and sunflower oils contain considerable amounts of *poly*unsaturated fats.

All foods that contain dietary fat are actually made up of mixtures of saturated and unsaturated (*mono*unsaturated and/or *poly*unsaturated) fatty acids. In fact, even dietary fats such as cooking oils

and margarine contain a mixture of these types of fatty acids. For example, 49 percent of the fat in butter is saturated, while 31 percent is unsaturated. Olive oil, well known for its *mono*unsaturated fat, which makes up 73 percent of the total fatty acid content, is a better choice, even though it also includes 13 percent saturated fat. You'll want to choose fats that contain more unsaturated fat than saturated fat. But the level of saturation of any fat can be altered by a process called hydrogenation.

What Is a Hydrogenated Fat?

Hydrogenation is a way to change unsaturated fatty acids to have a more saturated chemical structure. This is achieved by adding more hydrogen to the fatty acid molecule. Highly unsaturated vegetable oils are not stable enough for use in packaged foods. They develop "off flavors" in short periods of time. To increase "shelf life," some alteration such as hydrogenation of the oil is often necessary. Shortening made by blending hydrogenated vegetable oils, like coconut or palm oil, can improve flavor and extend the shelf life of packaged foods. When hydrogenated, vegetable oil margarine becomes solid and spreadable at room temperature, and when refrigerated properly, it maintains an acceptable flavor.

Another category of fats called "omega-3 fatty acids" is unique. These are highly polyunsaturated fatty acids found in fish, shellfish and plants from the sea. As a general rule, the higher the fat content of the seafood, the more omega-3 fatty acids it contains.

Research suggests that diets rich in omega-3 fatty acids may help reduce the risk for heart disease. Many health organizations recommend that we eat more fish and shellfish.

What Is Cholesterol?

Essential to life, cholesterol is produced by the body. In fact, the body makes 800 to 1,500 milligrams of cholesterol each day, which circulates through the bloodstream. Cholesterol has important functions in the body. It helps to produce certain hormones and is a vital part of your nervous system and brain.

A soft, waxy, fatlike substance, cholesterol is found *only* in animal foods. That means plant foods— grains, fruits, vegetables, nuts—do *not* contain cholesterol.

The cholesterol in the foods we eat is *dietary* cholesterol, while the cholesterol in our *blood* comes from two sources: the foods we eat and the body's own manufacturing process. For most people, dietary cholesterol from foods has only a small influence on blood cholesterol because the body controls the level in the bloodstream. Even so, health experts recommend that we limit the dietary cholesterol from our foods to 300 milligrams each day. The easiest way to do that is to learn which foods contain cholesterol.

The most concentrated sources of *dietary* cholesterol are organ meats, such as liver, brain and kidney. Egg yolk also contains a significant amount. The tables on pages 209–13 lists the cholesterol content of some familiar foods. Compare the different foods so you'll know the better choices.

What Are HDLs and LDLs?

Here is what happens to dietary cholesterol once it gets into the bloodstream. Substances called low-density lipoproteins (LDLs) carry cholesterol from the liver (where it is formed) to cells throughout the body. Excess cholesterol is deposited on artery walls. These deposits or "plaques" can build up over time and can contribute to coronary heart disease (CHD). Another blood cholesterol carrier called high-density lipoproteins (HDLs) carries the extra cholesterol away from the artery walls and back to the liver for reprocessing or removal from the body. HDLs help to prevent cholesterol build-up.

For some people, it may not be enough just to know their total blood cholesterol number. This is especially true for people whose total blood cholesterol is 240 milligrams per deciliter of blood or higher. A blood profile can determine the levels of LDLs and HDLs. This type of analysis may be advisable for those with borderline-high cholesterol levels (200–239 milligrams per deciliter of blood) plus two risk factors for CHD (for example, smoking and high blood pressure) or for people who already have CHD. Look at the chart on page 8 and make note of your CHD risk factors. A desirable LDL level is less than 130 milligrams per deciliter, while a desirable HDL level is above 35 milligrams per deciliter of blood.

A direct relationship exists between the total blood cholesterol level and the level of LDL. Three known causes of elevated LDL and blood cholesterol levels are:

- Genetic factors and family history

- A diet high in saturated fats and cholesterol

- Health conditions such as diabetes, diseases of the liver and kidney or an underactive thyroid.

A low level of HDL may indicate an increased risk of heart disease. Some possible causes of low HDL levels include lack of exercise, obesity, smoking and high blood cholesterol and/or triglycerides (another type of fat in the blood).

The next step is learning how to use this information about fat to change your eating habits.

Reducing Fat in Your Diet

Physicians, nutritionists and researchers have developed some guides to help you reduce the amount of fat and cholesterol you eat.

- Eat fewer high-fat foods. Eating less *visible* fat like lard, shortening or oil is important, but *hidden* fat is abundant too. Limiting fat intake may mean eating less ice cream, fewer chips and less creamy or cheesy mixed dishes. We need to be aware of the fat in food—its type and quantity—to make choices that will keep total fat intake and calories down.

- Eat smaller portions. Remember, just because a food is high in fat or cholesterol doesn't mean we can't eat it at all. It just means we should eat smaller servings, less often.

- Choose a cooking method that uses less fat. Broil, bake, roast, grill, poach, steam, stew or even microwave foods whenever possible. You can stir-fry, too, if you use small amounts of unsaturated oils.

- Use nonstick cookware. A nonstick skillet and one or two nonstick saucepans with a nonstick cooking spray can easily lessen the amounts of fat used in cooking.

- Choose meatless meals at least twice each week. Limiting the amount of meat, fish and poultry you eat can help reduce fat, particularly saturated fat, and increase fiber and complex carbohydrate when you trade meats for dried beans and peas, grains, vegetables and fruits. Try these foods in combinations. Just go easy on the margarine, mayonnaise and creamy sauces.

- Serve chicken, turkey or fish. Light-meat chicken and turkey are naturally low in fat, especially if you remove the skin. Most fish is also very lean. Even such higher-fat fish as salmon is as lean or leaner than poultry and lean beef. Some fish also have the added benefit of omega-3 fatty acids.

- Select lean cuts of meat and trim fat. Many leaner cuts of beef, pork and lamb are now available. Trim visible fat before cooking. (It's probably not a good idea to completely eliminate meats from the diet because they are important sources of many nutrients, among them are iron and vitamin B_{12}, that may be hard to get from other foods.)

- Use lowfat or skim milk products. Many milk products contain a great deal of fat, especially if they are made with whole milk or cream. Choose from the many low-fat and nonfat dairy products that are available. Look for skim milk, low-fat or skim milk cheeses and low-fat or nonfat yogurt. Don't eliminate dairy products entirely, because they provide the calcium we need for healthy bones.

- Limit added fats and oils to five to eight teaspoons per day. We're talking about how much butter you add to bread and the amount of dressing or mayonnaise you load on salads. Try nonfat and reduced-fat margarine and dressings. Remember, there's no need to give up fats completely. But we do need to be aware of how much we eat and limit portions or make substitutions wherever possible.

- Limit eggs to four per week. With 210 milligrams of cholesterol, one egg yolk supplies more than two-thirds the recommended daily limit. The good news is that egg whites have no cholesterol and in many cases can be used instead of whole eggs. For example, try omelets made with one whole egg and four egg whites or use an egg substitute.

Filling Up with Fiber

Although generations of grandmothers have long known the value of roughage in the diet, scientific interest in fiber has increased only in recent years.

In the 1960s, scientists found that rural Africans eating many foods loaded with fiber had a lower incidence of cancer of the colon (large intestine) than did Americans or Europeans living in industrialized civilizations.

Since the turn of the century, the amount of fiber we eat each day in the United States has declined. As new information emerges about the link between health and fiber, experts are recommending that we increase our intake. Fiber consumption is now "in style."

Fiber is part of the structure of plants. It is found in many foods containing complex carbohydrate, such as whole grain cereals and breads and many vegetables and fruits. Fiber is not found in meat or dairy products. According to scientists, *dietary* fiber is the nondigestible material that remains after plant foods pass through the intestinal tract.

It is not a single substance but a complex mixture of many.

Dietary fiber can be divided into two types: *soluble* and *insoluble* fiber. Soluble fiber, as its name suggests, dissolves in water. Insoluble fiber, what Grandma called roughage, does not dissolve in water. Some of the most important information to develop from recent research is the difference between these two kinds of fiber.

Insoluble fiber promotes regularity, and is being studied for its potential to reduce risks of colon and rectal cancers. But until recently, soluble fiber was practically ignored, largely because the role of soluble fiber in the diet just was not clear.

Some important effects of soluble fiber on the digestive and absorptive processes have been demonstrated, and soluble fiber may help to lower blood cholesterol when part of a low-fat diet. Soluble fiber shows promise in helping to control blood sugar levels in some diabetics, too. See below for a list of good sources of soluble and insoluble fiber.

Good Sources of Soluble and Insoluble Fiber

Mostly Soluble	Contains Both Soluble and Insoluble	Mostly Insoluble
Citrus fruits	Oat bran	Wheat bran
Citrus pectin	Whole-grain oats	Corn bran
Apple pectin	Carrots	Brown rice
	Apples	Cauliflower
	Potatoes	Bananas
	Broccoli	Nuts
		Lentils

Source: Compiled by General Mills, Inc., 1995.

The relationship of bran to dietary fiber is confusing. Bran, the coarse, outer layer of the whole grain kernel, is the major source of fiber in the grain. In addition to fiber, bran contains some starch, protein, vitamins, minerals and a small amount of fat. Depending on the grain source of the bran, it will contain different amounts of soluble and insoluble fiber.

Currently, there are no established recommended dietary allowances (RDAs) for fiber, but the daily value (DV) set by the Food and Drug Administration (FDA) is 25 grams of total dietary fiber each day. Translated into daily food choices, that means:

- Five or more servings of fruits and vegetables.

- Six or more servings of whole grain varieties of breads and cereals, and legumes (peas and beans) several times a day.

Putting It All Together

Fat, cholesterol and fiber are only three considerations for a healthful diet. We need more than forty different nutrients for good health, so even when we understand the facts about good nutrition, it may seem we need to be experts to come up with a plan. Fortunately, that work has already been done for us.

Back in the 1940s, we began to realize more fully the impact of diet on our health. Emerging from the Depression era when people regularly experienced food shortages, we saw a great number of people with diseases related to deficiencies of certain nutrients. To combat this national health problem, nutritionists devised a plan for daily eating that divided foods into groups according to similarity in nutrient content. Originally called the Basic Four Food Groups, the plan was recently revised and is now known as the Food Guide Pyramid. (See page 207 for more details.)

The **Bread, Cereal, Rice and Pasta Group** provides carbohydrate, iron and B vitamins (thiamine, riboflavin and niacin). Servings from this group include one ounce (about 3/4 cup) of breakfast cereal, one slice of bread, 1/2 cup cooked pasta or rice, and 1/2 cup cooked cereal. Everyone needs *six to eleven servings* of these foods daily.

The **Vegetable Group** is made up of just that—vegetables. This group gives us fiber, carbohydrate and vitamins A and C. One cup raw leafy vegetables, 1/2 cup cooked vegetables or 3/4 cup of tomato juice are some examples of servings. Eat *three to five servings* from this group each day.

The **Fruit Group** supplies primarily fiber, carbohydrate and vitamins A and C from fruit and juices. Everyone needs *two to four servings* of these foods each day. One medium piece of fruit, 1/2 cup of grapes or berries, 1/4 cup dried fruit, such as raisins, or 3/4 cup fruit juice are typical servings.

Iron, protein, niacin, vitamin B_6 and vitamin B_{12} (from animal sources only) come from the **Meat, Poultry, Fish, Dry Beans, Eggs and Nuts Group.** *Two to three servings* daily are enough for adults. One serving is two or three ounces of cooked lean protein (beef, poultry, fish), one egg, two tablespoons of peanut butter or 1/2 cup of cooked legumes (beans or peas).

We should eat *two to three servings* from the **Milk, Yogurt and Cheese Group** each day. This group provides the calcium, phosphorus, protein and vitamins A and D we need. One serving includes one cup of milk, one cup of yogurt, and 1 1/2 ounces of cheese. Young adults (to age twenty-four), pregnant women and those who are breast-feeding need three servings daily.

The **Fats, Oils and Sweets Group** provides fatty acids and vitamin E. But avoid eating too much from this group, especially if you're trying to lose weight.

When the food groups were first devised, nutrient *deficiencies* were a concern. Today, we're more likely to be getting too much of certain nutrients, rather than too little. By eating the recommended number of servings daily from the Food Guide Pyramid, you can ensure you will meet your needs for the many essential nutrients.

If you're not following the Food Guide Pyramid to the letter, at least remember to consider the content of fat, cholesterol and fiber of each food. Also, think about how much salt or sodium, sugar, calcium and iron you eat. We discuss these issues in the following pages.

Other Important Nutrients

Protein plays a role in many body processes and is vital to growth, maintaining and repairing body tissues. In addition to the foods you commonly think of as "protein" foods such as meats, cheese and eggs, protein is found in breads, cereals, dry beans and peas. Americans tend to eat more than twice the amount of protein we need, and experts think we should eat less. By limiting the number of servings and portion sizes to those we talked about earlier, you'll meet the recommendation.

You may have heard a lot about *calcium* because of its role in maintaining strong, healthy bones and teeth. Osteoporosis, a condition whereby bones become porous and brittle, threatens great numbers of older women in our country today. Along with several other factors, calcium deficiency may be a factor in the development of osteoporosis. There's speculation, too, that high blood pressure may result from too little calcium. Adolescent girls and adult women should be particularly careful to eat foods high in calcium. Dairy foods such as milk, cheese and yogurt are very good sources, although calcium is also found in dark green leafy vegetables, such as broccoli and collard greens, and in fish with edible bones, such as canned salmon and sardines.

Our bodies need *sodium* for proper kidney, nerve and muscle function as well as helping to control blood pressure. But in some people, too much *salt* (sodium chloride) and *sodium* may contribute to the development of high blood pressure. Although it's impossible to predict who will develop high blood pressure, and not everyone who does is affected by the amount of salt they eat, it's wise to keep sodium intake to a moderate level. Current U.S. averages estimate we eat 4,500 milligrams of sodium daily. According to the FDA, we should try to reduce our daily intake to about 2,400 milligrams. That's just more than one teaspoon of salt (about 2,300 milligrams of sodium). One way to reduce sodium intake is to use less salt at the table and in food preparation and only eat high sodium foods occasionally.

Another nutrient, *iron,* is necessary for oxygen transfer to body cells and, therefore, plays a vital role in how much energy we have. Iron-deficiency anemia (a disease from not enough iron) continues to be a health problem in the United States, particularly among women of child-bearing age who lose iron monthly through menstruation. Children, adolescents and members of low-income families are at high risk for iron deficiency also. Iron is getting even more attention lately as people eat less red meat in the interests of health. Choosing lean meats, however, can ensure that you get enough iron and still keep your fat intake in line. Other good sources of iron include dry beans and peas, iron-enriched cereals and whole grain products.

Sugar's reputation as a dietary "bad guy" is generally undeserved. The only health problem that sugar has been linked to is the development of dental cavities. And for those who are particularly vulnerable to cavities, especially children, limiting how much sugar they eat and how often they eat it is important. But it isn't only sugar; any carbohydrate food can cause tooth decay—even crackers or fruit—if you're not brushing properly. Brushing after meals and snacks helps to cleanse teeth by removing cavity-forming bacteria.

A Guide for Heart-Healthy Eating

Food Category	Choose More	Choose Less
Breads, cereals	Whole grain breads, whole wheat, pumpernickel, rye; bread sticks, English muffins, bagels, rice cakes, pita bread, Oatbran, oatmeal, whole grain cereals Saltines,* pretzels,* zwieback, plain popcorn	Croissants, butter rolls Cheese crackers, butter crackers
Rice, pasta	Rice, pasta	Egg noodles
Baked goods	Angel food cake	Frosted cakes, sweet rolls, pastries, doughnuts
Fruits	Fresh, frozen or dried fruits	Fruit pies, fruit desserts
Vegetables	Fresh or frozen vegetables	Vegetables prepared with butter, cream or cheese sauces
Meat, poultry, fish	Lean meats, skinless poultry, fish, shellfish	Fatty meats, organ meats, cold cuts, sausages, hot dogs
Beans, peas	Split peas, kidney beans, navy beans, lentils, soybeans, tofu	

Food Category	Choose More	Choose Less
Eggs	Egg whites; fat-free, cholesterol-free egg product	Egg yolks
Milk, cream	Skim milk, 1% milk, low-fat or fat-free buttermilk	Whole milk, 2% milk, half-and-half, whipped toppings, most nondairy creamers, sour cream, heavy (whipping) cream
Cheese	Nonfat or low-fat cottage cheese, nonfat or low-fat cheeses, farmer cheese	Whole milk cottage cheese, hard cheeses, cream cheese
Yogurt	Nonfat or low-fat yogurt	Whole milk yogurt
Frozen desserts	Ice milk, sherbet, nonfat or low-fat frozen yogurt	Ice cream
Fats, oils	Polyunsaturated or monounsaturated vegetable oils: sunflower, corn, soybean, olive, safflower, sesame, canola, cottonseed	Saturated fats: coconut oil, palm oil, palm kernel oil, lard, bacon fat
Spreads	Margarine or shortening made with polyunsaturated fat	Butter
Chocolate	Cocoa	Chocolate

*Reduced-sodium varieties

Source: Adapted from The American Heart Association Diet: An Eating Plan for Healthy Americans, American Heart Association.

Reading Nutrition Labels

As the American lifestyle continues to quicken in pace, and fewer people take time to prepare home-made foods, it becomes increasingly important to be able to read and understand the information food manufacturers provide about the nutritional content of their products. Once we learn how to read labels, we are better able to make more informed food choices.

The Nutrition Labeling and Education Act (NLEA), effective in 1994, made it mandatory by law for all packaged foods to carry a *Nutrition Facts* label. The nutrition label provides extensive information on the nutrients we want to know more about, such as fat, saturated fat, cholesterol, sodium and fiber.

Information about nutrients is listed in grams or milligrams based on specified serving sizes derived from the amount of foods people actually eat. This way NLEA labels are standardized to make product comparisons by nutrients easier. The Percent Daily Value, a measure of how a particular food stacks up when compared to an average diet of 2,000 calories per day, is listed for certain nutrients as well. See page 208 for more details.

All foods are required to list ingredients on the label in descending order of predominance by weight. For example, the *ingredient list* on a can of green beans might read, "Green beans, water, salt." That means that the can contains more green beans than water or salt, and more water than salt.

Also, the government sets standard definitions for terms used to describe product claims, such as *light, low fat, low sodium* and *high fiber.* If a can of green beans, for instance, is labeled "low sodium," it must meet the FDA guidelines for a "low-sodium" product. Now we can better understand the meaning of these claims and trust what we read on packages and in advertising. These claims can only be used if a food meets strict government definitions. Here are some of the meanings:

Label Claims

Label Claim	Definition (per serving)
Low Calorie	40 calories or less
Light or Lite	1/3 fewer calories OR 50 percent less fat than regular product; if more than half the calories are from fat, fat content must be reduced by 50 percent or more
Light in Sodium	50 percent less sodium than regular product
Fat Free	Less than 1/2 gram of fat
Low Fat	3 grams of fat or less fat
Cholesterol Free	Less than 2 milligrams of cholesterol and 2 grams or less saturated fat
Low Cholesterol	20 milligrams or less cholesterol and 2 grams or less saturated fat
Sodium Free	Less than 5 milligrams sodium
Very Low Sodium	35 milligrams or less sodium
Low Sodium	140 milligrams or less sodium
High Fiber	5 grams or more of fiber

Can a diet help reduce the risk for heart disease, cancer, or osteoporosis? Some food packages may now carry health claims. A health claim is a label statement that describes the relationship between a nutrient and a disease or health-related condition. A food must meet certain nutrient levels to make a health claim.

Seven types of health claims based on nutrient-disease relationships are permitted on food packages and are listed as follows:

Health Claims

A diet that is:	May help to reduce the risk of:
High in calcium	Osteoporosis (brittle bone disease)
High in fiber from fruits, vegetables and grain products	Cancer
High in fruits or vegetables (high in dietary fiber or vitamins A or C)	Cancer
High in fiber from fruits, vegetables and grain products	Heart disease
Low in fat	Cancer
Low in saturated fat and cholesterol	Heart disease
Low in sodium	High blood pressure (hy pertension)

Balancing Pleasure and Good Nutrition

While proper nutrition is vital to good health, let's not forget the pleasurable role that food plays in our lives. It may seem unfortunate that many of our favorite foods are high in fat, salt or sugar. Even so, in the context of a total diet, there's plenty of room to continue to enjoy these foods while eating healthfully. The bottom line is variety, balance and moderation—the basics of good nutrition.

Choosing a wide variety of foods helps to ensure that we're getting all the nutrients we need, while avoiding an excess of any one of them. Variety also helps to satisfy our taste buds through a wide choice of different foods with differing flavors.

In light of our food concerns today, balance helps us keep fat, cholesterol, salt and sugar in line with current recommendations. Simply put, balance means alternately eating foods low in fat, cholesterol, salt or sugar. "Perfect" foods aren't practical or necessary. What's important is how food choices balance out throughout the day.

Moderation focuses on both the amount of food you eat and the frequency with which you eat certain foods. Read food labels to learn recommended portion sizes of different foods. Then, remember, it's not necessary to give up any foods completely. Just reduce the amount you eat and the frequency to keep the fun in a healthful diet.

Exercise—Vital to a Healthful Lifestyle

What you eat is just one aspect of a healthful lifestyle. Many other factors also play a role. Among those factors, exercise takes a lead. A program of regular exercise can help you achieve or maintain a healthful body weight, reduced blood pressure and increased HDL levels. Regular exercise can help you maximize your potential for good health. It doesn't have to be a tedious chore or inconvenient, either!

Contrary to our nation's previous obsession with high-intensity exercises such as jogging, recent research indicates that moderate exercise can be very beneficial. Walking, playing golf, even gardening and housecleaning help firm muscles and burn extra calories.

New scientific studies suggest that adults benefit from 30 minutes or more of moderate-intensity physical activity on most, and preferably all, days of the week. Activity accumulated intermittently throughout the day can be added together to equal 30 minutes.

Of course, more active recreational pursuits such as dancing and tennis are even better. If you go that route, getting started is most often the difficult part of exercising. The following ideas can help you get past that crucial start-up point.

- Choose activities you enjoy.

- Vary exercises to avoid boredom and to fit with the season. Try swimming in summer and cross-country skiing in winter so you can enjoy the outdoors while keeping fit.

- Make a list of activities you can do alone or with family and friends. Flexibility helps you stay with your exercise program.

- Alternate aerobic activities with weight-bearing and flexibility exercises to meet your fitness needs. Walking and running fill two bills in that they are both weight-bearing and can be aerobic. Vigorous bike-riding and swimming are other aerobic exercises. Stretching exercises increase flexibility.

- Plan ahead to fit exercise into your schedule. If you leave it as a last-minute decision, you may never find the time.

- Choose a time that blends easily into your schedule so exercise becomes a regular routine.

Go Slowly for Greater Success

With eating habits or exercise, it's important to realize the value of gradual change. You've spent a lifetime developing your current habits, and if you expect to change all of them overnight, you may be undermining your chances for success. Try to take on one or two challenges and allow time to adjust. Small changes that add up to new overall habits are often the best way to guarantee success. Start by identifying major problem areas in your eating and exercise routines. Then prioritize those problems to determine which ones to tackle first.

Plan strategies that will help you overcome your hurdles. For example, if you eat too many high-fat foods and too few fruits, vegetables and complex carbohydrates, resolve to eat apple wedges, red pepper rings or pretzels instead of chips with your noontime sandwich. Change your standard breakfast to skim milk, cereal and fruit instead of doughnuts and pastries. Cut back on the amount of meat you eat by preparing meals that are combinations of vegetables, meat and complex carbohydrates such as mixed rice or pasta dishes. Remember, there's no need to completely forgo your less-healthful food favorites. You can continue to eat these foods occasionally.

Once you have control over the problem areas at the top of your list, move on to other areas that you think need improvement. If, even after reducing the amount of fat in your diet, you find that you're still eating a bit too much and consequently weigh more than you'd like to, work to reduce your portion sizes. Or, if regular exercise is a problem for you, focus on increasing your activity level, thereby burning up those extra calories.

Low-Fat, Low-Cholesterol Menus

To make health a part of your lifestyle, a commonsense blend of pleasure and good judgment may be the best approach. That way, you'll move closer to the three goals we spoke of at the beginning of this chapter—good health, a long life and happiness. To help you get started, here are eleven menus, designed for any occasion.

A FRUITFUL BRUNCH

Apple-Noodle Kugel (page 160)
Potato-Basil Scramble (page 116)
Blueberry Streusel Muffins (page 153)
Pumpkin-Fruit Bread (page 150)
Fruit cups
Foamy Refresher (page 192)

VEGETARIAN LUNCHEON

Gazpacho with Basil Cream (page 141)
Wheat Berry Salad (page 144)
Zucchini-Apricot Bread (page 150)
Lemon Meringue Cake with Strawberries
(page 188)

NOONTIME FUSION CONFUSION

Fish Burritos (page 102)
Oriental Coleslaw (page 170)
Tropical Tea (page 192)
Broiled Pineapple (page 184)

TEENS TAKE OVER

Almost Guacamole (page 30)
Spicy Tortilla Chips (page 34)
Whole Wheat Ratatouille Calzone (page 120)
Zesty Fruit Salad (page 171)
Vanilla ice milk with Chocolate Sauce
(page 202)
Chocolate Chip Cookies (page 204)

AT THE PARK

Tarragon Stuffed Eggs (page 38)
Sesame Chicken Salad (page 84)
Cut-up vegetables
Banana Muffins (page 155)
Peppermint Brownies (page 202)

BACKYARD BARBECUE

Vegetable dippers with Green Herb Dip
(page 30)
Gingered Flank Steak (page 50)
Two-Potato Salad with Dill Dressing
(page 171)
Corn on the cob
Frosted Banana Bars (page 203)

FAMILY FAVORITES

Herbed Pot Roast (page 48)
Mixed greens with Creamy Herb Dressing
(page 172)
Sour Cream Biscuits (page 155)
Apple-Cranberry Crisp (page 196)

CHILI LOVERS

Baked Buffalo Wings (page 42)
Three-Bean Chili (page 130)
Popovers (page 159)
Minty Lemonade Freeze (page 193)
Frozen fat-free yogurt with wafer cookies

BY THE HEARTH

> Chutney-glazed Yogurt Spread (page 32)
>
> Low-fat crackers
>
> Spicy Black Bean and Pork Stew (page 69)
>
> Mixed green salad with Apple-Horseradish Dressing (page 173)
>
> Southern Buttermilk Corn Bread (page 152)
>
> Orange and Currant Bread Pudding (page 198)

ELEGANT DINING

> Rice-stuffed Mushrooms (page 40)
>
> Salmon with Dilled Cucumbers (page 94)
>
> Sweet Potato–Apple Puree (page 165)
>
> Warm Greens with Balsamic Vinaigrette (page 175)
>
> Popovers (page 159)
>
> Blueberry Lime Torte (page 194)

COMPANY'S COMING

> Breadsticks with Caponata (page 32)
>
> Broiled Caribbean Swordfish (page 103)
>
> Spanish Gazpacho Rice (page 161)
>
> Spinach salad with Raspberry-Cilantro Dressing (page 172)
>
> Hard rolls
>
> Chocolate Swirl Cheesecake with Raspberry Topping (page 185)

From the menu "Company's Coming": Broiled Caribbean Swordfish (page 103), Spanish Gazpacho Rice (page 161), Spinach salad with Raspberry-Cilantro Dressing (page 172)

Planning Your Day

Health and nutrition experts recommend that we eat no more than 30 percent of our calories from fat. You can easily figure the percentage of fat in your daily diet. First, add the total number of calories consumed. Then, add up, separately, the number of grams of fat consumed. Multiply the number of grams of fat by nine (there are nine calories per gram of fat) for a total number of fat calories. Now, divide the number of fat calories by the total number of calories. Multiply that number by 100 to get the percent of calories that come from fat.

The menu plans that follow show you two examples of how to combine full days of healthful foods around menus from pages 21 and 23, for less than 30 percent of calories from fat. As you can see from these plans, each day's fat intake falls below that, yet neither is short of good food to eat.

Vegetarian Luncheon Daily Menu Plan

BREAKFAST

> 1 serving whole grain wheat flake cereal
>
> 1/2 medium banana
>
> 1 cup skim milk
>
> 1 Buttermilk–Toasted Oat Scone (page 156)
>
> Coffee or tea

LUNCH

> 1 serving Gazpacho with Basil Cream (page 141)
>
> 1 serving Wheat Berry Salad (page 144)
>
> 1 slice Zucchini-Apricot Bread (page 150)
>
> 1 piece Lemon Meringue Cake with Strawberries (page 188)
>
> 1 cup skim milk

DINNER

 1 serving Eggplant Lasagne (page 118)

 Mixed green salad with 2 tablespoons Creamy Herb Dressing (page 172)

 1 Popover (page 159)

 1 cup skim milk

 1 serving Broiled Pineapple (page 184)

SNACKS

 1 medium carrot

 1 serving Baked Pita Chips (page 34)

 2 tablespoons Hummus (page 35)

 1 cup tropical fruit juice blend

Calories 2245 (Calories from Fat 369); Fat 41 g (Saturated 9 g); Cholesterol 80 mg; Sodium 3700 mg; Carbohydrate 413 g; Protein 95 g

Percent fat calculation, using formula on page 23:

 41 g fat × 9 calories/g = 369 calories

 $$\frac{369 \text{ calories}}{2245 \text{ calories}} = 0.164$$

 0.164 × 100 = 16.4 = 16 percent calories from fat

By the Hearth Daily Menu Plan

BREAKFAST

 1 cup unsweetened strawberries

 1 Bran-Date Muffin (page 154)

 1 cup skim milk

 4 ounces tomato juice

LUNCH

 1 serving Bean Patties (page 125)

 1 serving Oriental Coleslaw (page 170)

 1 cup skim milk

 1 medium apple

DINNER

 2 tablespoons Chutney-glazed Yogurt Spread (page 32) with 4 low-fat crackers

 1 serving Spicy Black Bean and Pork Stew (page 69)

 Mixed green salad with 2 tablespoons Apple-Horseradish Dressing (page 173)

 1 piece Southern Buttermilk Corn Bread (page 152)

 12 ounces sparkling water

 1 serving Orange and Currant Bread Pudding (page 198)

 Decaf coffee or decaf tea

SNACKS

 1 medium pear

 1 cup lightly salted unbuttered air-popped popcorn

 1 serving Tropical Tea (page 192)

Calories 1710 (Calories from fat 270); Fat 30 g (Saturated 10 g); Cholesterol 82 mg; Sodium 2995 mg; Carbohydrate 312 g; Protein 87 g

Percent fat calculation, using formula on page 23:

 30 g fat × 9 calories/g = 270 calories

 $$\frac{270 \text{ calories}}{1710 \text{ calories}} = 0.158$$

 0.158 × 100 = 15.8 = 16 percent calories from fat

Feast on Your Favorites

Lowering the amount of fat and cholesterol in your diet does not mean that you have to eliminate all of your favorite recipes from your current repertoire. Simply review your recipes and reduce the amounts of fat-containing ingredients or substitute them with low-fat and low-cholesterol ingredients. Virtually all dairy products have low-fat versions available today. Many other products and ingredients do as well.

It also does not have to be an abrupt change that will be discouraging to you or your family. If you are using whole milk, start using 2 percent. Then in a few months, move to 1 percent, then to skim. If you use 2 percent now, move to 1 percent, etc.

Substitute a commercially available fat-free, cholesterol-free egg product, or, eliminate the yolks and just use egg whites for whole eggs. Refer to the substitution chart on page 212 for amounts. A drop or two of yellow food coloring added to recipes made with egg whites will give them the appearance of using whole eggs.

Reduce the amount of fat and use margarine or an unsaturated oil instead of butter in all cooking and baking. In many recipes, the oil, shortening or margarine that is used to sauté onions, garlic, mushrooms or chopped vegetables can be eliminated. Invest in a nonstick skillet and use nonstick cooking spray, water, broth, herb vinegar or wine instead of the fat. The White Sauce on page 178 is made with only half the margarine of a traditional white sauce and further reduces fat and cholesterol by using skim milk.

Baked products are a little trickier. The best thing to do is make small alterations until you achieve the product you want. Start by replacing the egg yolks with whites. Decrease the fat to the next even measurement. If a recipe calls for 1/2 cup margarine, try 1/3 cup and then go on to 1/4 cup the next time, if the product performed with 1/3 cup. It is unlikely that the fat can be decreased by more than one-half and still have good results. Or, substitute equal amounts of applesauce or strained prunes (baby food) for all of or part of the fat. We have already done the testing for you and have several bread recipes beginning on page 148 and several baked recipes throughout the Delicious Desserts chapter.

Reduce the amount of fat-containing particulates (like nuts, olives, cheese or chocolate) in your recipes and grate or chop them into smaller pieces so they will distribute further. We successfully use a small amount of miniature chocolate chips in both the Chocolate Chip Cookies (page 204) and the Cocoa-Oatmeal Cookies (page 206). Although they contain no cholesterol, nuts are high in fat and can easily be reduced or left out of most recipes.

The recipes in this book were not developed to be low-sodium, but we added only enough salt to give acceptable flavor. You can do the same thing with your recipes. Do not add salt if the recipe uses other ingredients that contain sodium. If several ingredients are high in sodium, use the low-sodium version of one of the ingredients. Or, just get in the habit of using the low-sodium version of a high-sodium product, like soy sauce.

Recipe Make-over

The Blueberry Streusel Muffin recipe on page 153 is a reduced-fat version of our traditional recipe that appears below. We have marked up the recipe to show you the changes we made for this book. These simple adjustments reduced the fat in each muffin by half and eliminated the cholesterol altogether.

Blueberry Streusel Muffins

12 MUFFINS

Streusel Topping (right)

1 cup *skim* milk

1/4 cup ~~vegetable oil~~ *unsweetened applesauce*

1/2 teaspoon vanilla

~~1 large egg~~ *1/4 cup fat-free cholesterol-free egg product or 2 egg whites*

2 cups all-purpose or whole wheat flour

1/3 cup sugar

3 teaspoons baking powder

1/2 teaspoon salt

1 cup fresh or canned (drained) blueberries*

Heat oven to 400°. Grease bottoms only of 12 medium muffin cups, 2 1/2 × 1 1/4 inches, with shortening, or line with paper baking cups. Prepare Streusel Topping; set aside.

Beat milk, ~~oil~~ *applesauce*, vanilla and egg *product* in large bowl. Stir in flour, sugar, baking powder and salt all at once just until flour is moistened (batter will be lumpy). Fold in blueberries. Divide batter evenly among muffin cups. Sprinkle each with about 2 teaspoons topping.

Bake 20 to 25 minutes or until golden brown. Immediately remove from pan to wire rack. Serve warm if desired.

STREUSEL TOPPING

2 tablespoons firm margarine or butter

1/4 cup all-purpose flour

2 tablespoons packed brown sugar

1/4 teaspoon ground cinnamon

Cut margarine into flour, brown sugar and cinnamon in medium bowl, using pastry blender or crisscrossing 2 knives, until crumbly.

*3/4 cup frozen (thawed and well drained) blueberries can be substituted for the fresh or canned blueberries.

Nutrition for 1 original Blueberry Streusel Muffin

Calories 195; Fat 8 g (Saturated 1g); Cholesterol 20 mg;

Nutrition for 1 revised Blueberry Streusel Muffin

Calories 155; Fat 4 g (Saturated 1 g); Cholesterol 0 mg

NUTRITION SYMBOLS

Every recipe in the book meets at least one of the fat or cholesterol nutritional criteria described at the right, and most meet both a fat and cholesterol criteria. Most recipes also meet the low-calorie criteria as well. It is unrealistic to expect each dish, or even each meal, to meet all nutritional guidelines. This chapter gives you the information you need to use the nutrition analysis provided with each recipe to put together a healthy eating plan for yourself or your family.

Low-Calorie

Recipes have 350 or fewer calories per serving with the exception of desserts. Low-calorie dessert recipes have 250 or fewer calories per serving.

Low-Fat

Recipes have 3 or fewer grams of fat per serving.

Moderate-Fat

Recipes have from 4 to 10 grams of fat per serving.

Low-Cholesterol

Recipes have 20 or fewer milligrams of cholesterol per serving.

Moderate-Cholesterol

Recipes have from 21 to 60 milligrams of cholesterol per serving.

2

Appetizers and Snacks

- Eat fruits and vegetables (steamed or uncooked) or pretzels in place of chips and crackers.

- If you do eat chips and crackers, always read the labels carefully on commercial snack products. Look for items without animal fats (lard or tallow) or saturated fats. And, even the lower-fat products can have more calories than you'd expect.

- Make use of the reduced-fat and fat-free mayonnaise, salad dressing and dairy products when making dips and spreads.

- Remember that herbs and spices give wonderful flavor to dips and spreads—without adding salt, as dry mixes can.

- Avoid fried foods, such as deep-fried cheese curds, breaded vegetables or potato skins.

Baked Pita Chips (page 34), Black Bean Dip (page 35), Hummus (page 35), Chicken Satay (page 44)

Almost Guacamole

ABOUT 1 1/2 CUPS DIP

Peas, sun-dried tomatoes and fat-free mayonnaise help stretch one avocado into guacamole for a crowd. The fresh taste of cilantro makes its own special mark.

4 sun-dried tomato halves (not oil-packed)

2/3 cup frozen (thawed) peas

1/2 cup fat-free mayonnaise or salad dressing

1/4 teaspoon salt

Dash of pepper

2 tablespoons lemon juice

1 medium onion, coarsely chopped (1/2 cup)

1 medium ripe avocado, cut into chunks

2 tablespoons lightly packed fresh cilantro leaves, if desired

Cover tomato halves with boiling water; let stand 5 minutes. Drain and chop.

Place peas, mayonnaise, salt, pepper, lemon juice and onion in blender or food processor. Cover and blend on medium-high speed, stopping blender occasionally to scrape sides, until smooth. Add avocado and cilantro. Cover and blend on medium-high speed until smooth.

Spoon dip into small bowl. Stir in tomatoes.

2 Tablespoons:		% Daily Value:	
Calories	40	Vitamin A	0%
Calories from fat	2	Vitamin C	4%
Fat, g	0	Calcium	0%
Saturated, g	0	Iron	2%
Cholesterol, mg	0	**Diet Exchanges:**	
Sodium, mg	190	Vegetable	1
Carbohydrate, g	5		
Dietary Fiber, g	1		
Protein, g	1		

Green Herb Dip

ABOUT 1 CUP DIP

3/4 cup plain fat-free yogurt

1/4 cup fat-free mayonnaise or salad dressing

1/4 teaspoon salt

1/2 cup lightly packed watercress leaves

1/2 cup lightly packed fresh parsley leaves

1/4 cup lightly packed fresh basil leaves

1 green onion, cut into 1-inch pieces

Raw vegetables for dipping, if desired

Place yogurt, mayonnaise and salt in blender or food processor. Add watercress, parsley, basil and onion. Cover and blend on medium-high speed about 30 seconds, stopping blender occasionally to scrape sides, until leaves are finely chopped.

Spoon dip into serving dish. Cover and refrigerate about 1 hour or until slightly thickened and chilled. Serve with vegetables.

2 Tablespoons:		% Daily Value:	
Calories	20	Vitamin A	4%
Calories from fat	0	Vitamin C	10%
Fat, g	0	Calcium	6%
Saturated, g	0	Iron	2%
Cholesterol, mg	0	**Diet Exchanges:**	
Sodium, mg	180	Vegetable	1
Carbohydrate, g	4		
Dietary Fiber, g	0		
Protein, g	1		

Green Herb Dip

Chutney-glazed Yogurt Spread

ABOUT 2 CUPS SPREAD

Thick Yogurt (below)

1/2 cup shredded fat-free Cheddar cheese (2 ounces)

1 tablespoon finely chopped green onion

1/2 teaspoon curry powder

1 jar (9 ounces) chutney (1 cup)

2 tablespoons chopped green onions

Plain toast rounds or crackers, if desired

Prepare Thick Yogurt. Mix yogurt, cheese, 1 tablespoon onion and the curry powder. Spread mixture about 3/4 inch thick in shallow 8-inch serving dish. Top with chutney. Sprinkle with 2 tablespoons onions. Serve with toast rounds.

THICK YOGURT

4 cups plain fat-free yogurt (without gelatin)

Line 6-inch strainer with basket-style paper coffee filter or double-thickness cheesecloth. Place strainer over bowl. Spoon yogurt into strainer. Cover strainer and bowl and refrigerate at least 12 hours, draining liquid from bowl occasionally.

2 Tablespoons:		% Daily Value:	
Calories	55	Vitamin A	0%
Calories from fat	0	Vitamin C	4%
Fat, g	0	Calcium	14%
Saturated, g	0	Iron	0%
Cholesterol, mg	5	**Diet Exchanges:**	
Sodium, mg	75	Lean meat	1/2
Carbohydrate, g	10	Fruit	1/2
Dietary Fiber, g	0		
Protein, g	4		

Caponata

ABOUT 3 CUPS DIP

1 tablespoon olive or vegetable oil

1 medium onion, chopped (1/2 cup)

2 cloves garlic, finely chopped

7 cups chopped peeled eggplant (1 1/2 pounds)

1 medium tomato, chopped (3/4 cup)

2 tablespoons chopped fresh or 2 teaspoons dried basil leaves

2 tablespoons red wine vinegar

1/4 teaspoon salt

1/4 teaspoon pepper

Pita bread wedges or Baked Pita Chips (page 34)

Heat oil in 10-inch nonstick skillet over medium heat. Cook onion and garlic in oil, stirring occasionally, until onion is tender. Stir in eggplant and tomato. Cook 8 to 10 minutes, stirring frequently, until eggplant is very tender.

Stir in basil, vinegar, salt and pepper. Cover and refrigerate about 2 hours or until cool. Serve with pita bread wedges.

2 Tablespoons:		% Daily Value:	
Calories	15	Vitamin A	0%
Calories from fat	10	Vitamin C	0%
Fat, g	1	Calcium	0%
Saturated, g	0	Iron	0%
Cholesterol, mg	0	**Diet Exchanges:**	
Sodium, mg	25	Free food	
Carbohydrate, g	2		
Dietary Fiber, g	0		
Protein, g	0		

Caponata, Chutney-glazed Yogurt Spread

Chips without Guilt

The best way to keep from eating high-fat snacks is to have something on hand that fits the bill when you need to munch. Whether you eat them alone or with any of the dips on pages 30 to 35, these tasty low-fat chips will satisfy the crunchy munchies!

SPICY TORTILLA CHIPS

12 SERVINGS (4 TO 5 CHIPS EACH)

2 tablespoons margarine, melted

1/2 teaspoon chili powder

8 corn or fat-free flour tortillas (6 to 8 inches in diameter)

Heat oven to 400°. Mix margarine and chili powder; brush on one side of tortillas. Cut each into 6 to 8 wedges. Place in 2 ungreased jelly roll pans, 15 1/2 × 10 1/2 × 1 inch. Bake uncovered 8 to 10 minutes or until crisp and golden brown; cool. (Tortillas will continue to crisp as they cool.)

1 Serving:		% Daily Value:	
Calories	55	Vitamin A	2%
Calories from fat	20	Vitamin C	0%
Fat, g	2	Calcium	2%
Saturated, g	0	Iron	2%
Cholesterol, mg	0	**Diet Exchanges:**	
Sodium, mg	55	Starch/bread	1/2
Carbohydrate, g	9		
Dietary Fiber, g	1		
Protein, g	1		

BAKED PITA CHIPS

8 SERVINGS (8 CHIPS EACH)

4 whole wheat pita breads (6 inches in diameter)

Heat oven to 400°. Cut around edge of each pita bread to separate layers. Cut each layer into 8 wedges. Place in single layer on 2 ungreased cookie sheets.

Bake about 9 minutes or until crisp and light brown; cool.

1 Serving:		% Daily Value:	
Calories	80	Vitamin A	0%
Calories from fat	10	Vitamin C	0%
Fat, g	1	Calcium	0%
Saturated, g	0	Iron	4%
Cholesterol, mg	0	**Diet Exchanges:**	
Sodium, mg	160	Starch/bread	1
Carbohydrate, g	17		
Dietary Fiber, g	2		
Protein, g	3		

Black Bean Dip

ABOUT 2 CUPS DIP

1 tablespoon canned chopped green chilies

1 small onion, chopped (1/4 cup)

1 clove garlic, crushed

1 can (15 ounces) black beans, rinsed and drained

1/2 cup plain fat-free yogurt

1/2 teaspoon ground cumin

1/4 teaspoon salt

Low-fat chips or crackers, if desired

Place chilies, onion, garlic and beans in blender or food processor. Cover and blend on medium-high speed, stopping blender occasionally to scrape sides, until almost smooth.

Spoon dip into small bowl. Stir in yogurt, cumin and salt. Serve cold, or heat in 1 1/2-quart saucepan over medium heat, stirring frequently, until hot. Serve with chips.

2 Tablespoons:		% Daily Value:	
Calories	30	Vitamin A	0%
Calories from fat	0	Vitamin C	2%
Fat, g	0	Calcium	2%
Saturated, g	0	Iron	4%
Cholesterol, mg	0	**Diet Exchanges:**	
Sodium, mg	95	Vegetable	1
Carbohydrate, g	7		
Dietary Fiber, g	1		
Protein, g	2		

Hummus

2 CUPS DIP

1 can (15 to 16 ounces) garbanzo beans, drained and liquid reserved

1/2 cup sesame seed

1 clove garlic, crushed

3 tablespoons lemon juice

1 teaspoon salt

Chopped fresh parsley

Pita bread wedges, Baked Pita Chips (page 34), low-fat crackers or raw vegetables for dipping, if desired

Place reserved bean liquid, the sesame seed and garlic in blender or food processor. Cover and blend on high speed until mixed. Add beans, lemon juice and salt. Cover and blend on high speed, stopping blender occasionally to scrape sides if necessary, until uniform consistency.

Spoon dip into serving dish. Sprinkle with parsley. Serve with pita bread wedges.

2 Tablespoons:		% Daily Value:	
Calories	65	Vitamin A	0%
Calories from fat	25	Vitamin C	2%
Fat, g	3	Calcium	2%
Saturated, g	0	Iron	6%
Cholesterol, mg	0	**Diet Exchanges:**	
Sodium, mg	190	Vegetable	1
Carbohydrate, g	7	Fat	1
Dietary Fiber, g	1		
Protein, g	3		

Stuffed Pattypan Squash

8 SERVINGS (2 TINY SQUASH EACH)

16 tiny pattypan squash (about 1 1/2 inches in diameter)*

1/2 cup soft bread crumbs (3/4 slice bread)

1 teaspoon chopped fresh or 1/4 teaspoon dried thyme leaves

1/4 teaspoon salt

2 green onions, finely chopped

1 tablespoon grated reduced-fat Parmesan cheese blend

Heat oven to 350°. Heat 1 inch water to boiling in 2-quart saucepan. Add squash. Cook 6 to 8 minutes or until crisp-tender; drain. Cut off stem ends. Hollow out squash; reserve squash shells. Finely chop squash pulp.

Mix squash pulp, bread crumbs, thyme, salt and onions. Spoon 1 heaping teaspoon squash mixture into each squash shell. Sprinkle with cheese. Place in ungreased square pan, 9 × 9 × 2 inches. Bake uncovered 10 to 12 minutes or until hot.

*8 small pattypan squash (about 2 1/2 inches in diameter) can be substituted for the tiny squash. Spoon 1 heaping tablespoon squash mixture into each squash shell.

1 Serving:		% Daily Value:	
Calories	15	Vitamin A	2%
Calories from fat	0	Vitamin C	2%
Fat, g	0	Calcium	2%
Saturated, g	0	Iron	2%
Cholesterol, mg	0	**Diet Exchanges:**	
Sodium, mg	95	Free food	
Carbohydrate, g	3		
Dietary Fiber, g	0		
Protein, g	1		

Fruit Kabobs with Nutmeg Dipping Sauce

6 SERVINGS (2 KABOBS AND 2 1/2 TABLESPOONS SAUCE EACH)

1 container (8 ounces) vanilla fat-free yogurt

1/4 cup sliced fresh strawberries

1/4 cup reduced-fat sour cream

1/2 teaspoon ground nutmeg

2 tablespoons maple-flavored syrup or packed brown sugar

4 cups mixed fresh fruit (sliced bananas, cantaloupe chunks, green or red seedless grapes, sliced peaches, pineapple chunks or whole strawberries)

Fresh mint leaves, if desired

Place yogurt, sliced strawberries, sour cream, nutmeg and maple syrup in blender or food processor. Cover and blend on low speed, stopping blender occasionally to scrape sides if necessary, until smooth. Spoon into serving dish. Cover and refrigerate about 1 hour or until chilled.

Thread fruit onto twelve 6-inch skewers, alternating colors and types of fruit and placing a mint leaf after each piece. Serve with nutmeg sauce.

1 Serving:		% Daily Value:	
Calories	115	Vitamin A	12%
Calories from fat	10	Vitamin C	64%
Fat, g	1	Calcium	8%
Saturated, g	1	Iron	4%
Cholesterol, mg	5	**Diet Exchanges:**	
Sodium, mg	30	Fruit	1 1/2
Carbohydrate, g	24		
Dietary Fiber, g	2		
Protein, g	3		

Fruit Kabobs with Nutmeg Dipping Sauce

Vegetable Potstickers

10 SERVINGS (3 POTSTICKERS EACH)

1 Serving:		% Daily Value:	
Calories	75	Vitamin A	0%
Calories from fat	10	Vitamin C	2%
Fat, g	1	Calcium	4%
Saturated, g	0	Iron	4%
Cholesterol, mg	0	**Diet Exchanges:**	
Sodium, mg	270	Starch/bread	1
Carbohydrate, g	14		
Dietary Fiber, g	1		
Protein, g	3		

1 1/2 cups fat-free chicken broth

1 medium onion, finely chopped (1/2 cup)

1 medium stalk celery, finely chopped (1/2 cup)

1/2 cup thinly sliced cabbage

1/2 cup chopped mushrooms

1 teaspoon grated gingerroot

2 cloves garlic, finely chopped

1 teaspoon low-sodium soy sauce

1 teaspoon dark sesame oil

1/2 package (16-ounce size) wonton skins (30 skins)

Heat 3/4 cup of the broth to boiling in 10-inch nonstick skillet over medium-high heat. Stir in onion, celery, cabbage, mushrooms, gingerroot and garlic. Cook 5 to 8 minutes, stirring frequently and adding more broth if vegetables begin to stick, until vegetables are tender. Remove from heat. Stir in soy sauce and sesame oil. Remove vegetable mixture from skillet. Wash and dry skillet.

Brush edges of one wonton skin with water. Place 1 teaspoon vegetable mixture on center of skin. Fold skin in half over filling and pinch edges to seal. Make creases in sealed edges to form pleats on one side of each potsticker. Repeat with remaining wonton skins and vegetable mixture.

Spray skillet with nonstick cooking spray. Heat skillet over medium heat. Cook potstickers in skillet, pleat sides up, about 1 minute or until bottoms are light brown. Add remaining 3/4 cup broth. Cover and cook 5 to 8 minutes or until most of liquid is absorbed.

Tarragon Stuffed Eggs

4 SERVINGS (2 EGG HALVES EACH)

1/2 cup fat-free cholesterol-free egg product

1/4 cup chopped watercress or fresh spinach

2 tablespoons fat-free mayonnaise or salad dressing

2 teaspoons chopped shallot

1/2 teaspoon chopped fresh or 1/4 teaspoon dried tarragon leaves

1/2 teaspoon white wine vinegar

1/8 teaspoon salt

Dash of pepper

4 hard-cooked eggs

Thinly sliced ripe olives, if desired

Spray 8-inch nonstick skillet with nonstick cooking spray. Heat skillet over medium-high heat. Pour egg product into skillet. As egg product begins to set at bottom and side, gently lift cooked portions with spatula so that thin, uncooked portion can flow to bottom. Avoid constant stirring. Cook 1 to 2 minutes or until thickened throughout but still moist; cool.

Mash cooked egg product with fork. Stir in remaining ingredients except hard-cooked eggs and olives. Cut hard-cooked eggs lengthwise in half; discard yolks. Fill egg whites with watercress mixture, mounding lightly. Place on serving plate. Cover and refrigerate up to 24 hours. Garnish with olives.

1 Serving:		% Daily Value:	
Calories	35	Vitamin A	2%
Calories from fat	0	Vitamin C	2%
Fat, g	0	Calcium	2%
Saturated, g	0	Iron	2%
Cholesterol, mg	0	**Diet Exchanges:**	
Sodium, mg	260	Lean meat	1/2
Carbohydrate, g	3	Vegetable	1
Dietary Fiber, g	0		
Protein, g	6		

Cheesy Frittata Squares

4 SERVINGS (4 SQUARES EACH)

1/4 cup fat-free chicken broth

1 clove garlic, finely chopped

1 small onion, chopped (1/4 cup)

3/4 cup shredded reduced-fat sharp Cheddar cheese (3 ounces)

2 tablespoons finely chopped fresh parsley

1 teaspoon chopped fresh or 1/4 teaspoon dried dill weed

1/8 teaspoon pepper

1/8 teaspoon red pepper sauce

1 slice whole wheat bread, crumbled

1 can (10 ounces) artichoke hearts, drained and chopped

1 container (8 ounces) fat-free cholesterol-free egg product (1 cup)

Heat oven to 325°. Spray square pan, $8 \times 8 \times 2$ inches, with nonstick cooking spray. Heat broth to boiling in 8-inch nonstick skillet over medium heat. Cook garlic and onion in broth 3 to 5 minutes, stirring constantly, until liquid has evaporated.

Spoon onion mixture into medium bowl. Stir in remaining ingredients until well mixed. Spoon into pan.

Bake uncovered about 30 minutes or until set and light brown. Cool 5 minutes. Cut into 16 squares.

1 Serving:		% Daily Value:	
Calories	150	Vitamin A	8%
Calories from fat	35	Vitamin C	10%
Fat, g	4	Calcium	22%
Saturated, g	2	Iron	16%
Cholesterol, mg	10	**Diet Exchanges:**	
Sodium, mg	370	Starch/bread	1
Carbohydrate, g	17	Lean meat	1
Dietary Fiber, g	4		
Protein, g	15		

Rice-stuffed Mushrooms

4 SERVINGS (3 MUSHROOMS EACH)

12 large mushrooms

1/4 cup fat-free chicken broth

1 large onion, finely chopped (1 cup)

1 clove garlic, finely chopped

1 tablespoon dry sherry or apple juice

1/2 cup soft whole wheat bread crumbs (3/4 slice bread)

1/2 cup cooked wild or white rice

2 tablespoons chopped fresh parsley

2 tablespoons grated reduced-fat Parmesan cheese blend

1/4 teaspoon salt

Set oven control to broil. Remove stems from mushroom caps; set stems aside. Place mushroom caps, stem sides down, in ungreased jelly roll pan, 15 1/2 × 10 1/2 × 1 inch. Broil with tops about 4 inches from heat about 5 minutes or until mushrooms begin to release moisture. Remove mushrooms from pan; drain on paper towels. Finely chop mushroom stems.

Heat broth to boiling in 10-inch nonstick skillet over medium-high heat. Stir in onion, garlic, mushroom stems and sherry. Cook 8 to 10 minutes, stirring frequently, until onion is tender. Stir in remaining ingredients. Cook, stirring frequently, until hot.

Place mushroom caps, stem sides up, in jelly roll pan. Spoon onion mixture into caps, mounding slightly. Broil with tops about 4 inches from heat 3 to 5 minutes or until onion mixture is light brown.

1 Serving:		% Daily Value:	
Calories	80	Vitamin A	0%
Calories from fat	20	Vitamin C	6%
Fat, g	2	Calcium	6%
Saturated, g	1	Iron	8%
Cholesterol, mg	2	**Diet Exchanges:**	
Sodium, mg	260	Starch/bread	1
Carbohydrate, g	14		
Dietary Fiber, g	2		
Protein, g	4		

Ginger Shrimp Kabobs

4 SERVINGS (3 SKEWERS EACH)

12 uncooked large shrimp in shells

1 tablespoon grated gingerroot

2 tablespoons lime juice

2 teaspoons low-sodium soy sauce

1 teaspoon dark sesame oil

1/4 teaspoon crushed red pepper

3 cloves garlic, finely chopped

1 medium red bell pepper, cut into
    12 one-inch squares

12 small whole mushrooms

6 green onions, cut into 1-inch pieces

1 medium yellow bell pepper, cut into
    12 one-inch squares

Peel shrimp. (If shrimp are frozen, do not thaw; peel in cold water.) Make a shallow cut lengthwise down back of each shrimp; wash out vein.

Mix gingerroot, lime juice, soy sauce, sesame oil, red pepper and garlic in glass or plastic container. Stir in shrimp until well coated. Cover and refrigerate 1 hour.

Heat grill or set oven to broil. Remove shrimp from marinade; reserve marinade. Alternate red bell pepper, mushroom, shrimp, onion and yellow bell pepper on each of 12 six-inch skewers.* Brush lightly with marinade. Grill or broil about 4 inches from heat about 6 minutes, turning once, until shrimp are pink and vegetables are crisp-tender. Discard any remaining marinade.

*If using bamboo skewers, soak in water at least 30 minutes before using to prevent burning.

1 Serving:		% Daily Value:	
Calories	65	Vitamin A	24%
Calories from fat	20	Vitamin C	65%
Fat, g	2	Calcium	2%
Saturated, g	0	Iron	8%
Cholesterol, mg	40	**Diet Exchanges:**	
Sodium, mg	230	Lean meat	1/2
Carbohydrate, g	7	Vegetable	1
Dietary Fiber, g	1		
Protein, g	6		

Baked Buffalo Wings

4 SERVINGS (6 DRUMETTES AND 2 TABLESPOONS SAUCE EACH)

Who says you can't eat those favorite restaurant wings? Our skinless version is even complete with a low-fat dipping sauce.

2 pounds chicken drumettes (about 24)

2 tablespoons honey

2 tablespoons ketchup

2 tablespoons red pepper sauce

1 tablespoon Worcestershire sauce

Blue Cheese Dipping Sauce (right)

Paprika

Heat oven to 350°. Line jelly roll pan, 15 1/2 × 10 1/2 × 1 inch, with aluminum foil. Remove skin from chicken.

Mix honey, ketchup, pepper sauce and Worcestershire sauce in plastic bag with zipper top. Add chicken. Seal bag and refrigerate 5 minutes, turning occasionally. Prepare Blue Cheese Dipping Sauce.

Place chicken in pan; sprinkle with paprika. Bake about 30 minutes or until juice of chicken is no longer pink when centers of thickest pieces are cut. Serve with sauce.

BLUE CHEESE DIPPING SAUCE

1/3 cup fat-free cottage cheese

1/2 teaspoon white wine vinegar

2 tablespoons low-fat milk

1 tablespoon crumbled blue cheese

1/8 teaspoon white pepper

1 clove garlic, finely chopped

Place cottage cheese, vinegar, milk, half of the blue cheese, the white pepper and garlic in blender or food processor. Cover and blend on low speed, stopping blender occasionally to scrape sides if necessary, until smooth and creamy. Spoon into serving dish. Stir in remaining blue cheese. Cover and refrigerate until serving time.

1 Serving:		% Daily Value:	
Calories	215	Vitamin A	6%
Calories from fat	35	Vitamin C	2%
Fat, g	4	Calcium	6%
Saturated, g	2	Iron	8%
Cholesterol, mg	70	**Diet Exchanges:**	
Sodium, mg	340	Starch/bread	1
Carbohydrate, g	14	Lean meat	2 1/2
Dietary Fiber, g	0		
Protein, g	31		

Baked Buffalo Wings, Vegetable Potstickers (page 38)

Chicken Satay

12 APPETIZERS

An authentic, Asian satay consists of marinated meat or seafood grilled on skewers and served with a sauce. Hoisin and plum sauce replace the high-fat peanut sauce that usually accompanies satay.

1 pound boneless, skinless chicken breast halves

1/3 cup hoisin sauce

1/3 cup plum sauce

2 tablespoons sliced green onions

1 tablespoon grated gingerroot

2 tablespoons dry sherry or fat-free chicken broth

2 tablespoons white vinegar

Trim fat from chicken. Cut chicken into 1/2-inch strips. Mix remaining ingredients in large glass or plastic bowl. Add chicken; toss to coat. Cover and refrigerate 2 hours.

Set oven control to broil. Remove chicken from marinade; drain, reserving marinade. Thread 2 pieces chicken on each of 12 ten-inch skewers.* Place on rack in broiler pan. Broil with tops 3 to 4 inches from heat about 8 minutes, turning once, until no longer pink in center. Heat marinade to boiling in 1-quart saucepan. Serve with chicken.

*If using bamboo skewers, soak in water at least 30 minutes before using to prevent burning.

1 Appetizer:		% Daily Value:	
Calories	65	Vitamin A	0%
Calories from fat	10	Vitamin C	2%
Fat, g	1	Calcium	0%
Saturated, g	0	Iron	2%
Cholesterol, mg	20	**Diet Exchanges:**	
Sodium, mg	40	Lean meat	1
Carbohydrate, g	5	Vegetable	1
Dietary Fiber, g	0		
Protein, g	9		

Chicken Terrine

16 SERVINGS

Serve thinly sliced with crackers, or slice 1/2 inch thick and serve as a first course with a dollop of the Green Herb Dip (page 30) on top.

1/4 cup chopped fresh parsley

1 1/2 pounds boneless, skinless chicken breast halves

2 tablespoons chopped shallots

1 tablespoon chopped fresh or 1 teaspoon dried thyme leaves

1 tablespoon vegetable oil

1 teaspoon salt

2 egg whites

1 small red bell pepper, chopped (1/2 cup)

Heat oven to 350°. Line loaf pan, 8 1/2 × 4 1/2 × 2 1/2 inches, with aluminum foil. Sprinkle parsley in bottom of pan.

Trim fat from chicken. Cut chicken into 1-inch pieces. Place chicken in food processor. Cover and process until coarsely ground. Add remaining ingredients except bell pepper. Cover and process until smooth. Stir in bell pepper. Spread in pan.

Cover pan tightly with aluminum foil. Bake 1 hour; remove foil. Bake 20 to 30 minutes longer or until meat thermometer inserted in center reads 180°. Cover and let stand 1 hour.

Refrigerate at least 3 hours. Invert onto serving platter. Remove pan and foil.

1 Serving:		% Daily Value:	
Calories	55	Vitamin A	2%
Calories from fat	20	Vitamin C	6%
Fat, g	2	Calcium	0%
Saturated, g	0	Iron	2%
Cholesterol, mg	25	Diet Exchanges:	
Sodium, mg	160	Lean meat	1
Carbohydrate, g	0		
Dietary Fiber, g	0		
Protein, g	9		

Spicy Cocktail Meatballs

3 DOZEN APPETIZERS

These south-of-the-border meatballs made with ground lean turkey scream party food!

2 jalapeño chilies*
1 pound lean ground turkey
2 egg whites
1 small onion, finely chopped (1/4 cup)
1/2 cup dry bread crumbs
1/4 cup shredded fat-free Monterey Jack
    or Cheddar cheese (1 ounce)
1/4 cup low-fat milk
1 teaspoon salt
1/4 teaspoon pepper
1/2 cup salsa
1 can (8 ounces) tomato sauce

Heat oven to 400°. Remove stems, seeds and membranes from chilies; chop chilies. Mix chilies, turkey, egg whites, onion, bread crumbs, cheese, milk, salt and pepper. Shape mixture into 1-inch balls. Arrange meatballs, sides not touching, in ungreased rectangular pan, $13 \times 9 \times 2$ inches.

Bake uncovered 15 to 20 minutes or until turkey is no longer pink. Heat salsa and tomato sauce in 1-quart saucepan, stirring occasionally, until hot. Place meatballs in chafing dish or serving dish. Pour salsa mixture over meatballs, or serve it on the side for dipping.

*2 tablespoons canned chopped green chilies can be substituted for the jalapeño chilies.

1 Appetizer:		% Daily Value:	
Calories	40	Vitamin A	4%
Calories from fat	20	Vitamin C	6%
Fat, g	2	Calcium	2%
Saturated, g	1	Iron	2%
Cholesterol, mg	10	Diet Exchanges:	
Sodium, mg	150	Lean meat	1/2
Carbohydrate, g	2		
Dietary Fiber, g	0		
Protein, g	3		

Meaty Main Dishes

3

- Use nonstick cookware and nonstick cooking spray so less added fat is needed in cooking.

- Reduce pan juices to the desired consistency and concentration of flavor instead of making floury and fat-laden sauces and gravies. But first, remove the fat from the pan juices by either using a fat separator or refrigerating juices, then skimming off the congealed fat from the top.

- Select lean cuts of meat and trim off all visible fat before cooking. When buying ground beef, choose extralean.

- Rib cuts of beef, pork, veal and lamb are fatty; loin cuts are leaner. Beef and veal flank and round cuts are relatively lean; leg and shoulder cuts should be examined for leanness before buying.

- Baste meats with their own juices or broth rather than butter or margarine.

Broiled Herb Steak (page 49), Buttery Herb Couscous (page 165), Green salad with Curried Yogurt Dressing (page 173)

Herbed Pot Roast

10 SERVINGS

Here's a traditional pot roast for the whole family, with enough for leftovers.

1 Serving:		% Daily Value:	
Calories	275	Vitamin A	82%
Calories from fat	35	Vitamin C	16%
Fat, g	4	Calcium	6%
Saturated, g	1	Iron	20%
Cholesterol, mg	65	**Diet Exchanges:**	
Sodium, mg	120	Starch/bread	2
Carbohydrate, g	37	Lean meat	2
Dietary Fiber, g	5	Vegetable	1
Protein, g	28		

3-pound lean beef boneless rump roast

1/2 teaspoon coarsely ground pepper

2 cloves garlic, finely chopped

1 cup dry red wine or beef broth

1 1/2 cups water

1/4 cup chopped fresh parsley

1 tablespoon chopped fresh or 1 teaspoon dried thyme leaves

1/2 teaspoon beef bouillon granules

5 whole cloves

3 bay leaves

10 small new potatoes (1 1/2 pounds)

5 medium carrots (3/4 pound), cut in half

4 large parsnips (1 pound), peeled and cut into eighths

2 medium onions, cut into eighths

Heat oven to 325°. Trim fat from beef. Mix pepper and garlic; rub on beef. Place in Dutch oven. Add wine, water, parsley, thyme, bouillon granules, cloves and bay leaves. Heat to boiling; reduce heat. Cover and simmer 2 1/2 hours.

Turn beef over. Add remaining ingredients. (Add water if necessary.) Cover and simmer 45 to 60 minutes or until beef and vegetables are tender. Remove cloves and bay leaves. Serve beef and vegetables with pan juices.

London Broil

4 SERVINGS

1 pound lean beef flank steak

2 medium onions, thinly sliced

1/4 teaspoon salt

1 tablespoon vegetable oil

1 teaspoon lemon juice

1/4 teaspoon salt

1/4 teaspoon pepper

2 cloves garlic, finely chopped

Trim fat from beef. Cut diamond pattern 1/8 inch deep into both sides of beef. Spray 10-inch non-stick skillet with nonstick cooking spray. Heat skillet over medium-high heat. Cook onions and 1/4 teaspoon salt in skillet about 4 minutes, stirring frequently, until light brown; keep warm. Mix remaining ingredients; brush half of the mixture on beef.

Set oven control to broil. Spray broiler pan rack with nonstick cooking spray. Place beef on rack in broiler pan. Broil with top about 3 inches from heat about 12 minutes for medium (160°), turning after 6 minutes and brushing with remaining garlic mixture. Cut beef across grain at slanted angle into thin slices. Serve with onions.

1 Serving:		% Daily Value:	
Calories	205	Vitamin A	0%
Calories from fat	100	Vitamin C	2%
Fat, g	11	Calcium	2%
Saturated, g	3	Iron	12%
Cholesterol, mg	60	**Diet Exchanges:**	
Sodium, mg	320	Lean meat	3
Carbohydrate, g	5	Vegetable	1
Dietary Fiber, g	1		
Protein, g	23		

Trim fat from beef. Place beef on large piece of plastic wrap. Mix remaining ingredients; brush on both sides of beef. Fold plastic wrap over beef and secure tightly. Refrigerate at least 5 hours but no longer than 24 hours.

Set oven control to broil. Spray broiler pan with non-stick cooking spray. Place beef on rack in broiler pan. Broil with top about 3 inches from heat 16 to 20 minutes for medium (160°), turning after 8 minutes. Cut beef across grain at slanted angle into 1/4-inch slices.

1 Serving:		% Daily Value:	
Calories	135	Vitamin A	0%
Calories from fat	45	Vitamin C	0%
Fat, g	5	Calcium	0%
Saturated, g	1	Iron	12%
Cholesterol, mg	55	**Diet Exchanges:**	
Sodium, mg	350	Lean meat	2 1/2
Carbohydrate, g	1		
Dietary Fiber, g	0		
Protein, g	21		

Broiled Herb Steak

8 SERVINGS

2-pound lean beef bone-in top round steak, about 1 inch thick

1 tablespoon chopped fresh or 1 teaspoon dried basil leaves

2 tablespoons reduced-sodium soy sauce

1 tablespoon vegetable oil

1 tablespoon ketchup

2 teaspoons chopped fresh or 1/2 teaspoon dried oregano leaves

1/2 teaspoon salt

1/2 teaspoon coarsely ground pepper

1 clove garlic, finely chopped

Swiss Steak

6 SERVINGS

1 1/2-pound beef boneless round, tip or chuck steak, about 3/4 inch thick

3 tablespoons all-purpose flour

1 teaspoon ground mustard (dry)

1/2 teaspoon salt

2 teaspoons vegetable oil

1 can (16 ounces) whole tomatoes, undrained

2 cloves garlic, finely chopped

1 cup water

1 large onion, sliced

1 large green bell pepper, sliced

Trim fat from beef. Mix flour, mustard and salt. Sprinkle one side of beef with half of the flour mixture; pound in. Turn beef and pound in remaining flour mixture. Cut beef into 6 serving pieces.

Heat oil in 10-inch nonstick skillet over medium heat. Cook beef in oil about 15 minutes, turning once, until brown. Add tomatoes and garlic, breaking up tomatoes. Heat to boiling; reduce heat. Cover and simmer about 1 1/4 hours or until beef is tender.

Add water, onion and bell pepper. Heat to boiling over heat; reduce heat. Cover and simmer 5 to 8 minutes or until vegetables are tender.

1 Serving:		% Daily Value:	
Calories	165	Vitamin A	6%
Calories from fat	45	Vitamin C	24%
Fat, g	5	Calcium	2%
Saturated, g	1	Iron	14%
Cholesterol, mg	55	**Diet Exchanges:**	
Sodium, mg	340	Lean meat	2
Carbohydrate, g	10	Vegetable	2
Dietary Fiber, g	2		
Protein, g	22		

Gingered Flank Steak

4 SERVINGS

1 pound lean beef flank steak

1/3 cup lemon juice

2 tablespoons honey

1 tablespoon reduced-sodium soy sauce

2 teaspoons grated gingerroot or 1 teaspoon ground ginger

2 cloves garlic, crushed

Trim fat from beef. Cut diamond pattern 1/8 inch deep into both sides of beef. Mix remaining ingredients in shallow glass or plastic dish. Place beef in dish; turn to coat both sides. Cover and refrigerate at least 8 hours but no longer than 24 hours, turning beef occasionally.

Set oven control to broil. Remove beef from marinade; reserve marinade. Spray broiler pan rack with nonstick cooking spray. Place beef on rack in broiler pan. Broil with top about 3 inches from heat about 12 minutes for medium (160°), turning after 6 minutes and brushing frequently with marinade. Discard any remaining marinade. Cut beef across grain at slanted angle into thin slices.

1 Serving:		% Daily Value:	
Calories	210	Vitamin A	0%
Calories from fat	70	Vitamin C	4%
Fat, g	8	Calcium	0%
Saturated, g	3	Iron	12%
Cholesterol, mg	60	**Diet Exchanges:**	
Sodium, mg	210	Starch/bread	1/2
Carbohydrate, g	11	Lean meat	3
Dietary Fiber, g	0		
Protein, g	23		

Gingered Flank Steak, Two-Potato Salad with Dill Dressing (page 171), Frosted Banana Bars (page 203)

Southwest Fajitas

4 SERVINGS

Plain fat-free yogurt replaces sour cream. If you have to have guacamole on your fajitas, try a little Almost Guacamole (page 30).

1 pound lean beef flank steak or skirt steak

1/4 cup lime juice

2 teaspoons chili powder

1 teaspoon ground cumin

2 cloves garlic, crushed

4 fat-free flour tortillas (10 inches in diameter)

1/2 cup salsa

1/2 cup plain fat-free yogurt

Chopped cilantro

Trim fat from beef. Pierce beef with fork in several places. Mix lime juice, chili powder, cumin and garlic in shallow glass or plastic dish. Place beef in dish; turn to coat both sides. Cover and refrigerate at least 4 hours but no longer than 24 hours, turning beef occasionally.

Heat oven to 325°. Wrap tortillas in aluminum foil. Heat in oven about 15 minutes or until warm. Remove from oven; keep wrapped.

Set oven control to broil. Spray broiler rack with nonstick cooking spray. Remove beef from marinade; discard marinade. Place beef on rack in broiler pan. Broil with top about 3 inches from heat about 12 minutes for medium (160°), turning after 6 minutes. Slice beef diagonally across grain at slanted angle into very thin slices.

Place one-fourth of the beef slices, 2 tablespoons of the salsa and 2 tablespoons of the yogurt on center of each tortilla. Fold one end of tortilla up about 1 inch over beef mixture; fold right and left sides over folded end, overlapping. Fold down remaining end. Serve with additional salsa and yogurt and sprinkle with cilantro if desired.

1 Serving:		% Daily Value:	
Calories	325	Vitamin A	36%
Calories from fat	80	Vitamin C	18%
Fat, g	9	Calcium	20%
Saturated, g	1	Iron	22%
Cholesterol, mg	50	**Diet Exchanges:**	
Sodium, mg	720	Starch/bread	2
Carbohydrate, g	33	Lean meat	3
Dietary Fiber, g	3		
Protein, g	31		

Meat Loaf

8 SERVINGS

Lean ground turkey and old-fashioned oats help cut fat and retain moistness in this tasty version of the all-family favorite.

3/4 pound extralean ground beef

3/4 pound lean ground turkey

1/2 cup old-fashioned oats

1/2 cup tomato puree

2 tablespoons chopped fresh parsley

1/2 teaspoon Italian seasoning

1/2 teaspoon salt

1/4 teaspoon pepper

1 small onion, chopped (1/4 cup)

1 clove garlic, finely chopped

Heat oven to 350°. Mix all ingredients thoroughly. Press mixture evenly in ungreased loaf pan, 8 1/2 × 4 1/2 × 2 1/2 or 9 × 5 × 3 inches. Bake uncovered 1 1/4 to 1 1/2 hours or until no longer pink in center and juice is clear.

1 Serving:		% Daily Value:	
Calories	180	Vitamin A	2%
Calories from fat	90	Vitamin C	4%
Fat, g	10	Calcium	2%
Saturated, g	3	Iron	10%
Cholesterol, mg	55	**Diet Exchanges:**	
Sodium, mg	240	Lean meat	3
Carbohydrate, g	6	Vegetable	1
Dietary Fiber, g	1		
Protein, g	18		

Spicy Burgers

4 SERVINGS

1 pound extralean ground beef

1/2 teaspoon chili powder

1/2 teaspoon pepper

1/4 teaspoon salt

1/4 teaspoon ground red pepper (cayenne)

1 clove garlic, finely chopped

Mix all ingredients thoroughly. Shape mixture into 4 patties, each 1/2 inch thick. Heat 10-inch nonstick skillet over medium-high heat. Place patties in skillet; reduce heat to medium. Cover and cook 6 to 8 minutes, turning once, until no longer pink in center and juice is clear.

1 Serving:		% Daily Value:	
Calories	♦ 170	Vitamin A	2%
Calories from fat	70	Vitamin C	0%
Fat, g	8	Calcium	0%
Saturated, g	3	Iron	12%
Cholesterol, mg	65	**Diet Exchanges:**	
Sodium, mg	190	Lean meat	3
Carbohydrate, g	1		
Dietary Fiber, g	0		
Protein, g	24		

Veal Stew Gremolata

4 SERVINGS (ABOUT 1 1/4 CUPS EACH)

Gremolata is an Italian garnish—or seasoning—made from parsley, lemon peel and garlic. Serve this dish with crusty bread.

1 pound lean veal shoulder

1 teaspoon vegetable oil

3/4 cup finely chopped onion

1/4 cup finely chopped carrot

1/4 cup finely chopped celery

1 clove garlic, crushed

1/2 cup dry red wine or beef broth

1 tablespoon chopped fresh or 1 teaspoon dried basil leaves

1/4 teaspoon salt

1 large bell pepper, cut into wedges

8 ounces mushrooms, cut in half

1 can (15 ounces) tomato puree

Gremolata (right)

Trim fat from veal. Cut veal into 1-inch pieces. Heat oil in nonstick Dutch oven over medium-high heat. Cook veal, onion, carrot, celery and garlic in oil 3 to 4 minutes, stirring frequently, until veal is brown.

Stir in remaining ingredients except Gremolata. Heat to boiling; reduce heat to low. Cover and cook 50 to 60 minutes, stirring occasionally, until veal is tender. Stir in Gremolata just before serving.

GREMOLATA

3 tablespoons finely chopped fresh parsley

1 tablespoon grated lemon peel

1 teaspoon finely chopped garlic

Mix all ingredients.

1 Serving:		% Daily Value:	
Calories	185	Vitamin A	30%
Calories from fat	45	Vitamin C	42%
Fat, g	5	Calcium	6%
Saturated, g	2	Iron	16%
Cholesterol, mg	70	**Diet Exchanges:**	
Sodium, mg	630	Starch/bread	1/2
Carbohydrate, g	19	Lean meat	2
Dietary Fiber, g	4	Vegetable	2
Protein, g	20		

Veal with Asparagus

4 SERVINGS (WITH ABOUT 1/2 CUP VEGETABLE MIXTURE EACH)

1 teaspoon vegetable oil

1 tablespoon finely chopped shallot

1 clove garlic, finely chopped

3/4 pound thin slices lean veal round steak or veal for scaloppini

1 cup sliced mushrooms (3 ounces)

1/3 cup dry white wine

2 teaspoons chopped fresh or 1/2 teaspoon dried thyme leaves

12 ounces asparagus spears, cut into 1-inch pieces*

Heat oil in 10-inch nonstick skillet over medium-high heat. Cook shallot and garlic in oil, stirring frequently, until garlic is golden; reduce heat to medium. Add veal. Cook about 3 minutes, turning once, until light brown.

Stir in remaining ingredients. Heat to boiling; reduce heat. Cover and simmer about 12 minutes, stirring occasionally, until asparagus is crisp-tender.

*1 package (10 ounces) frozen asparagus cuts, thawed, can be substituted for the fresh asparagus.

1 Serving:		% Daily Value:	
Calories	110	Vitamin A	4%
Calories from fat	35	Vitamin C	8%
Fat, g	4	Calcium	2%
Saturated, g	1	Iron	6%
Cholesterol, mg	55	**Diet Exchanges:**	
Sodium, mg	50	Lean meat	1 1/2
Carbohydrate, g	4	Vegetable	1
Dietary Fiber, g	1		
Protein, g	15		

Veal with Asparagus

Stuffed Veal Chops with Cider Sauce

4 SERVINGS (WITH ABOUT 1/4 CUP SAUCE EACH)

4 lean veal loin chops, 1 inch thick (about 6 ounces each)

1 cup soft bread crumbs (1 1/2 slices bread)

1/2 cup chopped all-purpose apple

2 tablespoons chopped fresh parsley

2 tablespoons apple cider

1/4 teaspoon salt

1/8 teaspoon ground allspice

1 small onion, chopped (1/4 cup)

Cider Sauce (right)

Trim fat from veal. Cut slit in each veal chop to form a pocket. Mix remaining ingredients except Cider Sauce. Fill each pocket with about 1/3 cup stuffing mixture.

Spray 10-inch nonstick skillet with nonstick cooking spray. Heat skillet over medium-high heat. Cook veal in skillet about 7 minutes, turning once, until brown; reduce heat to low. Cover and cook 20 to 25 minutes or until veal is tender. Remove veal to serving platter; keep warm.

Reserve 1/2 cup pan juices in skillet (strain, if necessary). Prepare Cider Sauce. Serve with veal.

CIDER SAUCE

Reserved pan juices

1 cup apple cider

1/2 cup apple brandy or apple cider

2 tablespoons white wine vinegar

1 teaspoon cornstarch

1 tablespoon water

Add enough water to pan juices to measure 1/2 cup; pour into skillet. Stir cider, brandy and vinegar into skillet. Heat to boiling. Boil 6 to 8 minutes or until mixture is reduced to about 1 cup. Mix cornstarch and water; stir into cider mixture. Heat to boiling, stirring constantly. Boil and stir 1 minute.

1 Serving:		% Daily Value:	
Calories	200	Vitamin A	0%
Calories from fat	35	Vitamin C	2%
Fat, g	4	Calcium	4%
Saturated, g	1	Iron	8%
Cholesterol, mg	60	**Diet Exchanges:**	
Sodium, mg	240	Starch/bread	1
Carbohydrate, g	26	Lean meat	1 1/2
Dietary Fiber, g	1	Fruit	1/2
Protein, g	16	Vegetable	1

Low-Fat Marinades and Rubs

Marinades and rubs add flavor and interest to meats, poultry and fish. The acid (vinegar, lemon juice) in marinades also helps tenderize the meat. Because of that acid, be sure to marinate in nonreactive containers such as glass or plastic bowls or resealable plastic bags. Each of these flavorful low-fat combinations is enough for one pound of meat, or four servings.

GARLIC MARINADE

ABOUT 1/2 CUP MARINADE

2 tablespoons olive or vegetable oil

4 cloves garlic, finely chopped

1 tablespoon chopped fresh or
  1 teaspoon dried rosemary
  leaves, crushed

1 tablespoon water

2 teaspoons low-sodium soy sauce

1/2 teaspoon ground mustard

3 tablespoons red or white wine vinegar, dry sherry or apple juice

Heat oil in 10-inch skillet over medium-high heat. Cook garlic in oil, stirring frequently, until golden. Stir in rosemary, water, soy sauce and mustard; remove from heat. Stir in vinegar; cool. Use to marinate 1 pound beef, pork or chicken; bake, broil or grill meat.

1 Tablespoon:		% Daily Value:	
Calories	30	Vitamin A	0%
Calories from fat	25	Vitamin C	0%
Fat, g	3	Calcium	0%
Saturated, g	0	Iron	0%
Cholesterol, mg	0	**Diet Exchanges:**	
Sodium, mg	85	Free food	
Carbohydrate, g	1		
Dietary Fiber, g	0		
Protein, g	0		

(Continued on Next Page)

Citrus Marinade

About 1/2 cup marinade

1 tablespoon chopped fresh or 1 teaspoon dried basil leaves

3 tablespoons orange juice

2 tablespoons lemon juice

2 tablespoons olive or vegetable oil

1/2 teaspoon salt

1/4 teaspoon pepper

2 cloves garlic, finely chopped

1 Tablespoon:		% Daily Value:	
Calories	30	Vitamin A	0%
Calories from fat	25	Vitamin C	2%
Fat, g	3	Calcium	0%
Saturated, g	0	Iron	0%
Cholesterol, mg	0	**Diet Exchanges:**	
Sodium, mg	130	Free food	
Carbohydrate, g	1		
Dietary Fiber, g	0		
Protein, g	0		

Mix all ingredients. Use to marinate 1 pound pork, chicken or fish; bake, broil or grill meat.

Mustard Marinade

About 1/3 cup marinade

2 tablespoons water

2 tablespoons lemon juice

1 tablespoon olive or vegetable oil

1 tablespoon Dijon mustard

1/4 teaspoon pepper

1 Tablespoon:		% Daily Value:	
Calories	30	Vitamin A	0%
Calories from fat	25	Vitamin C	0%
Fat, g	3	Calcium	0%
Saturated, g	0	Iron	0%
Cholesterol, mg	0	**Diet Exchanges:**	
Sodium, mg	40	Free food	
Carbohydrate, g	1		
Dietary Fiber, g	0		
Protein, g	0		

Mix all ingredients. Use to marinate 1 pound beef, pork or chicken; bake, broil or grill meat.

Mexican Rub

2 teaspoons vegetable oil

1 tablespoon ground red chilies or chili powder

2 teaspoons dried oregano leaves

1/2 teaspoon ground cumin

1/2 teaspoon ground coriander

1/8 teaspoon salt

1 Serving:		% Daily Value:	
Calories	25	Vitamin A	6%
Calories from fat	25	Vitamin C	0%
Fat, g	3	Calcium	0%
Saturated, g	0	Iron	2%
Cholesterol, mg	0	**Diet Exchanges:**	
Sodium, mg	90	Free food	
Carbohydrate, g	1		
Dietary Fiber, g	1		
Protein, g	0		

Rub oil on 1 pound beef or chicken. Mix remaining ingredients; rub on meat. Bake, broil or grill meat.

Herb Rub

2 teaspoons olive or vegetable oil

1 tablespoon dried tarragon leaves

2 teaspoons dried thyme leaves

1 1/2 teaspoons dried sage leaves, crumbled

1/2 teaspoon onion powder

1/4 teaspoon salt

1 Serving:		% Daily Value:	
Calories	20	Vitamin A	0%
Calories from fat	20	Vitamin C	0%
Fat, g	2	Calcium	0%
Saturated, g	0	Iron	2%
Cholesterol, mg	0	**Diet Exchanges:**	
Sodium, mg	130	Free food	
Carbohydrate, g	1		
Dietary Fiber, g	0		
Protein, g	0		

Rub oil on 1 pound beef, pork or chicken. Mix remaining ingredients; rub on meat. Bake, broil or grill meat.

Caribbean Pork Tenderloin

4 SERVINGS (ABOUT 1 CUP EACH)

The plantain, a less-sweet cousin of the banana, is a principal starch in the Caribbean. Tip: Partially freeze tenderloins to make it easier to slice them thinly.

2 lean pork tenderloins, about 1/2 pound each

1 teaspoon grated orange peel

1/2 cup orange juice

2 tablespoons chopped fresh cilantro

2 tablespoons lime juice

1/2 teaspoon cracked black pepper

2 cloves garlic, cut in half

1 teaspoon cornstarch

1/4 teaspoon salt

1 teaspoon vegetable oil

1 large ripe plantain, cut into 1/4-inch slices

Trim fat from pork. Cut pork across grain into 1/8-inch slices. Mix orange peel, orange juice, cilantro, lime juice, pepper and garlic in large glass or plastic bowl. Stir in pork. Cover and refrigerate 30 minutes.

Remove pork from marinade; drain, reserving marinade. Stir cornstarch and salt into marinade; set aside.

Heat oil in 10-inch nonstick skillet over medium-high heat. Cook pork in oil about 4 minutes, stirring frequently, until no longer pink. Stir in plantain. Cook 2 to 3 minutes, stirring frequently, until plantain is brown and slightly soft. Stir in marinade mixture. Heat to boiling, stirring constantly. Boil and stir 1 minute.

1 Serving:		% Daily Value:	
Calories	255	Vitamin A	8%
Calories from fat	45	Vitamin C	20%
Fat, g	5	Calcium	0%
Saturated, g	2	Iron	10%
Cholesterol, mg	65	**Diet Exchanges:**	
Sodium, mg	190	Starch/bread	1
Carbohydrate, g	29	Lean meat	2
Dietary Fiber, g	1	Fruit	1
Protein, g	25		

Mushroom-stuffed Pork Chops

4 SERVINGS (WITH ABOUT 1/3 CUP STUFFING EACH)

To lower fat grams, broth substitutes for the usual oil in which the mushrooms, garlic and onion are cooked.

4 pork loin chops, 1/2 to 3/4 inch thick (about 1 pound)

1 cup fat-free chicken broth

2 1/2 cups chopped mushrooms (7 ounces)

2 cloves garlic, finely chopped

1 medium onion, chopped (1/2 cup)

1/2 cup soft bread crumbs (3/4 slice bread)

2 tablespoons chopped fresh parsley

Heat oven to 350°. Trim fat from pork. Make a pocket in each pork chop by cutting into side of pork toward the bone.

Heat 1/2 cup of the broth to boiling in ovenproof Dutch oven over medium-high heat. Stir in mushrooms, garlic and onion. Cook 5 minutes, stirring frequently; remove from heat. Stir in bread crumbs and parsley. Fill pockets in pork with mushroom mixture; secure openings with toothpicks. Cool Dutch oven slightly; wipe clean.

Spray Dutch oven with nonstick cooking spray. Heat Dutch oven over medium-high heat. Cook pork in Dutch oven until brown on both sides. Add remaining 1/2 cup broth.

Cover and bake about 1 hour or until pork is tender. Remove toothpicks before serving.

1 Serving:		% Daily Value:	
Calories	240	Vitamin A	0%
Calories from fat	80	Vitamin C	4%
Fat, g	9	Calcium	4%
Saturated, g	3	Iron	14%
Cholesterol, mg	65	**Diet Exchanges:**	
Sodium, mg	350	Starch/bread	1
Carbohydrate, g	14	Lean meat	3
Dietary Fiber, g	1		
Protein, g	27		

Seasoned Pork Chops with Apples

4 SERVINGS (WITH 1/3 CUP VEGETABLE MIXTURE EACH)

4 pork loin or rib chops, about 1/2 inch thick (about 1 pound)

1/4 cup all-purpose flour

1 teaspoon chopped fresh or 1/2 teaspoon dried thyme leaves

1 teaspoon paprika

1/4 teaspoon pepper

1 1/2 cups fat-free chicken broth

2 cups sliced onions (about 1 large)

2 cups sliced cabbage

2 green apples, peeled and sliced

1/4 cup chopped fresh parsley

Trim fat from pork. Mix flour, thyme, paprika and pepper in plastic bag with zipper top. Add pork. Seal bag and shake until pork is well coated.

Heat oven to 350°. Spray ovenproof Dutch oven with nonstick cooking spray. Heat Dutch oven over medium-high heat. Cook pork in Dutch oven until brown on both sides. Remove pork from Dutch oven.

Add broth to Dutch oven; scrape bottom with wooden spoon to loosen any brown bits. Heat to boiling. Stir in onions and cabbage. Cook 5 minutes, stirring frequently. Top with pork and apples.

Cover and bake about 1 hour or until pork is tender. Sprinkle with parsley before serving.

1 Serving:		% Daily Value:	
Calories	225	Vitamin A	6%
Calories from fat	65	Vitamin C	20%
Fat, g	7	Calcium	4%
Saturated, g	2	Iron	12%
Cholesterol, mg	50	**Diet Exchanges:**	
Sodium, mg	330	Lean meat	2
Carbohydrate, g	22	Vegetable	2
Dietary Fiber, g	3	Fruit	1
Protein, g	21		

Seasoned Pork Chops with Apples

Chinese Pork and Pasta

4 SERVINGS (1 1/2 CUPS EACH)

Sesame oil is usually added for flavor, but we use it here to cook the meat due to the low amount of oil in the recipe. Spraying the wok first with nonstick cooking spray allows for the small amount of oil.

1/2 pound lean pork tenderloin

1 can (8 ounces) pineapple chunks in juice, drained and juice reserved

1 tablespoon soy sauce

1 teaspoon honey or packed brown sugar

2 cloves garlic, finely chopped

1 tablespoon cornstarch

4 ounces uncooked vermicelli

2 teaspoons dark sesame oil

1/4 cup fat-free chicken broth

1/2 medium onion, sliced

1 medium red bell pepper, seeded and chopped (1 cup)

4 large stalks bok choy, chopped

4 ounces Chinese pea pods, strings removed

Trim fat from pork. Cut pork into 1/4-inch slices. Mix pineapple juice, soy sauce, honey, garlic and cornstarch in medium glass or plastic bowl. Stir in pork. Cover and refrigerate 1 hour.

Cook and drain vermicelli as directed on package. Spray wok or 10-inch nonstick skillet with nonstick cooking spray. Heat wok over medium-high heat. Add oil; rotate wok to coat side. Add pork; stir-fry 2 minutes. Remove pork from wok.

Add broth, onion, bell pepper and bok choy to wok; stir-fry 6 minutes. Add pea pods, pineapple and vermicelli. Cook 2 minutes, stirring constantly. Add pork. Cook about 1 minute, stirring constantly, until sauce is thickened.

1 Serving:		% Daily Value:	
Calories	250	Vitamin A	32%
Calories from fat	45	Vitamin C	70%
Fat, g	5	Calcium	10%
Saturated, g	1	Iron	16%
Cholesterol, mg	35	**Diet Exchanges:**	
Sodium, mg	380	Starch/bread	2
Carbohydrate, g	36	Lean meat	1 1/2
Dietary Fiber, g	3	Vegetable	1
Protein, g	18		

Garlicky Pork with Basil

4 SERVINGS

3/4 pound lean pork tenderloin

1 teaspoon vegetable oil

1/4 cup chopped fresh or 1 tablespoon plus 1 teaspoon dried basil leaves

1/4 cup fat-free chicken broth

1/8 teaspoon ground red pepper (cayenne)

4 cloves garlic, finely chopped

Trim fat from pork. Cut pork crosswise into 8 serving pieces. Flatten each piece pork to 1/4-inch thickness between waxed paper or plastic wrap.

Heat oil in 10-inch nonstick skillet over medium-high heat. Cook pork in oil about 3 minutes, turning once, until brown. Stir in remaining ingredients. Heat to boiling; reduce heat. Cover and simmer about 5 minutes or until pork is slightly pink in center.

1 Serving:		% Daily Value:	
Calories	115	Vitamin A	0%
Calories from fat	35	Vitamin C	0%
Fat, g	4	Calcium	2%
Saturated, g	1	Iron	6%
Cholesterol, mg	50	**Diet Exchanges:**	
Sodium, mg	85	Lean meat	2
Carbohydrate, g	2		
Dietary Fiber, g	0		
Protein, g	18		

Pork Paprikash

4 SERVINGS (1 1/2 CUPS EACH)

8 ounces uncooked cholesterol-free wide noodles

1/2 pound lean pork tenderloin

1 cup fat-free chicken broth

1/2 large onion, sliced

2 cloves garlic, finely chopped

1 cup sliced mushrooms (3 ounces)

1 large carrot, sliced diagonally

1 1/2 teaspoons paprika

1 tablespoon cornstarch

1 cup reduced-fat sour cream

1 cup frozen green peas, thawed

1/4 cup chopped fresh parsley

2 teaspoons Worcestershire sauce

Cook and drain noodles as directed on package. Trim fat from pork. Cut pork into 1/2-inch cubes. Spray nonstick Dutch oven with nonstick cooking spray. Heat Dutch oven over medium-high heat. Cook pork in Dutch oven, stirring frequently, until brown. Add 1/2 cup of the broth; heat to boiling. Stir in onion, garlic, mushrooms, carrot and paprika.

Cook 10 to 12 minutes or until vegetables are tender. Stir cornstarch into sour cream; stir into pork mixture. Stir in the noodles, 1/2 cup broth and remaining ingredients; heat through.

1 Serving:		% Daily Value:	
Calories	395	Vitamin A	62%
Calories from fat	70	Vitamin C	12%
Fat, g	8	Calcium	12%
Saturated, g	4	Iron	24%
Cholesterol, mg	55	**Diet Exchanges:**	
Sodium, mg	350	Starch/bread	3
Carbohydrate, g	61	Lean meat	1
Dietary Fiber, g	6	Vegetable	1
Protein, g	26	Skim milk	1

Spicy Black Bean and Pork Stew

4 SERVINGS (ABOUT 1 1/3 CUPS EACH)

Wonderful flavors blend together in a healthy, hearty stew for those cold winter nights. Serve with a crisp green salad with Curried Yogurt Dressing (page 173) and crusty whole grain bread.

4 cups water

1/2 cup dried black beans (4 ounces)

2 ancho chilies

3/4 pound lean pork boneless shoulder

1/2 cup dry red wine or fat-free chicken broth

1 tablespoon chopped fresh or 1 teaspoon dried sage leaves

1 tablespoon chopped fresh or l teaspoon dried marjoram leaves

1/2 teaspoon salt

1/2 teaspoon ground cumin

1/4 teaspoon ground cinnamon

2 large tomatoes, peeled, seeded and chopped (1 1/2 cups)

1 medium onion, chopped (1/2 cup)

1 clove garlic, finely chopped

2 cups 1-inch cubes peeled butternut squash

1 medium red bell pepper, cut into 1-inch pieces

2 tablespoons chopped fresh cilantro

Heat water, beans and chilies to boiling in nonstick Dutch oven. Boil uncovered 2 minutes; remove from heat. Cover and let stand l hour.

Remove chilies; reserve. Heat beans to boiling; reduce heat. Cover and simmer 1 hour.

Seed and coarsely chop chilies. Trim fat from pork. Cut pork into 1-inch cubes. Stir pork, chilies and remaining ingredients except squash, bell pepper and cilantro into beans. Heat to boiling; reduce heat. Cover and simmer 30 minutes, stirring occasionally.

Stir in squash. Cover and simmer 30 minutes, stirring occasionally, until squash is tender. Stir in bell pepper and cilantro. Cover and simmer about 5 minutes or until bell pepper is crisp-tender.

1 Serving:		% Daily Value:	
Calories	305	Vitamin A	62%
Calories from fat	100	Vitamin C	88%
Fat, g	10	Calcium	8%
Saturated, g	4	Iron	20%
Cholesterol, mg	55	**Diet Exchanges:**	
Sodium, mg	310	Starch/bread	2
Carbohydrate, g	33	Lean meat	2
Dietary Fiber, g	8	Vegetable	1
Protein, g	26		

Vegetable and Ham Jambalaya

6 SERVINGS (ABOUT 1 1/3 CUPS EACH)

A spunky rendition of the Louisiana specialty with only two grams of fat per serving.

3/4 cup fat-free chicken broth

1 medium onion, chopped (1/2 cup)

2 cloves garlic, finely chopped

1/2 cup diced green bell pepper

1/2 cup diced celery

2 green onions, chopped

4 cups cooked rice

1 cup frozen whole kernel corn or green peas

1 cup cubed lean fully cooked ham (about 2/3 pound)

1 tablespoon tomato paste

1 teaspoon Worcestershire sauce

1/2 to 1 teaspoon red pepper sauce

1 can (16 ounces) whole peeled tomatoes, undrained

1/3 cup chopped fresh parsley

1/2 teaspoon salt

1/2 teaspoon pepper

Heat broth to boiling in Dutch oven. Stir in onion, garlic, bell pepper, celery and green onions. Cook 5 to 8 minutes, stirring frequently, until vegetables are tender.

Stir in remaining ingredients except parsley, salt and pepper, breaking up tomatoes. Heat to boiling; reduce heat to low. Cover and cook 30 minutes. Stir in parsley, salt, and pepper. Serve with additional red pepper sauce if desired.

1 Serving:		% Daily Value:	
Calories	220	Vitamin A	8%
Calories from fat	20	Vitamin C	26%
Fat, g	2	Calcium	4%
Saturated, g	1	Iron	16%
Cholesterol, mg	15	**Diet Exchanges:**	
Sodium, mg	730	Starch/bread	2
Carbohydrate, g	43	Lean meat	1/2
Dietary Fiber, g	3	Vegetable	2
Protein, g	10		

Ham with Cabbage and Apples

4 SERVINGS (WITH ABOUT 3/4 CUP CABBAGE MIXTURE EACH)

⌛ ◗ ♡

4 cups shredded cabbage

1 tablespoon packed brown sugar

1 tablespoon cider vinegar

1/8 teaspoon pepper

1 large green cooking apple, peeled, cored and cut into rings

1 medium onion, chopped (1/2 cup)

4 extralean ham steaks (about 3 ounces each)

Spray 10-inch nonstick skillet with nonstick cooking spray. Cook all ingredients except ham in skillet over medium heat about 5 minutes, stirring frequently, until apple is crisp-tender.

Place ham on cabbage mixture; reduce heat to low. Cover and cook about 10 minutes or until ham is hot.

1 Serving:		% Daily Value:	
Calories	175	Vitamin A	0%
Calories from fat	45	Vitamin C	34%
Fat, g	5	Calcium	4%
Saturated, g	1	Iron	10%
Cholesterol, mg	40	**Diet Exchanges:**	
Sodium, mg	930	Lean meat	2
Carbohydrate, g	18	Vegetable	1
Dietary Fiber, g	3	Fruit	1
Protein, g	17		

Lamb with Yogurt-Mint Sauce

4 SERVINGS
(WITH ABOUT 3 TABLESPOONS SAUCE EACH)

⌛ ◗ ♡

2/3 cup plain fat-free yogurt

1/4 cup firmly packed fresh mint leaves

2 tablespoons sugar

4 lamb loin chops, about 1 inch thick (about 1 pound)

Place yogurt, mint and sugar in blender or food processor. Cover and blend on medium speed, stopping blender occasionally to scrape sides, until leaves are finely chopped.

Set oven control to broil. Spray broiler pan rack with nonstick cooking spray. Trim fat from lamb. Place lamb on rack in broiler pan. Broil with tops about 3 inches from heat 12 to 14 minutes for medium (160°), turning after 6 minutes. Serve with sauce.

1 Serving:		% Daily Value:	
Calories	130	Vitamin A	0%
Calories from fat	35	Vitamin C	0%
Fat, g	4	Calcium	8%
Saturated, g	2	Iron	6%
Cholesterol, mg	40	**Diet Exchanges:**	
Sodium, mg	65	Starch/bread	1/2
Carbohydrate, g	9	Lean meat	2
Dietary Fiber, g	0		
Protein, g	15		

Moroccan Lamb Stew with Dried Fruits

6 SERVINGS (1 CUP STEW AND 1/2 CUP COUSCOUS EACH)

A rich, hearty stew naturally sweetened with apricots, prunes and raisins—all for a mere 4 grams of fat per serving.

1 pound lamb boneless shoulder

1 1/2 cups fat-free chicken broth

1 large onion, chopped (1 cup)

3 cloves garlic, finely chopped

1 tablespoon all-purpose flour

1 cup dry red wine or fat-free chicken broth

1 cup dried apricots

1/4 cup pitted prunes

1/4 cup raisins

1 teaspoon paprika

1 can (16 ounces) whole peeled tomatoes, undrained

1/3 cup chopped fresh parsley

3 cups hot cooked couscous

Trim fat from lamb. Cut lamb into cubes. Spray Dutch oven with nonstick cooking spray. Heat over medium-high heat. Cook lamb in Dutch oven, stirring frequently, until brown. Remove lamb from Dutch oven.

Add 1/2 cup of the broth to Dutch oven; heat to boiling. Stir in onion and garlic. Cook 3 minutes, stirring frequently. Stir in flour. Cook 1 minute, stirring constantly.

Stir in the lamb, remaining 1 cup broth, the wine, apricots, prunes, raisins, paprika and tomatoes, breaking up tomatoes. Heat to boiling; reduce heat. Cover and simmer 45 minutes. Stir in parsley. Serve over couscous.

1 Serving:		% Daily Value:	
Calories	295	Vitamin A	24%
Calories from fat	35	Vitamin C	16%
Fat, g	4	Calcium	6%
Saturated, g	1	Iron	20%
Cholesterol, mg	35	**Diet Exchanges:**	
Sodium, mg	560	Starch/bread	1
Carbohydrate, g	52	Lean meat	1 1/2
Dietary Fiber, g	5	Vegetable	1
Protein, g	18	Fruit	2

Moroccan Lamb Stew with Dried Fruits

4

Poultry and Fish

- Chicken, turkey, Cornish hens and pheasant are less fatty than duck and goose. Turkey is a bit leaner than chicken, and white meat has somewhat less fat and cholesterol than dark meat.

- Remove all visible fat before cooking. Most of poultry fat is in the skin, making it easier to remove than red meat fat, which tends to be marbled throughout. Although it isn't necessary to remove the poultry skin before cooking, as little is absorbed into the meat, it should be removed before eating.

- When buying ground turkey or chicken, look for packages that state lean or ground breast.

- Fin fish and shellfish are generally lower in fat than meats and poultry. Shellfish are higher than fin fish in cholesterol (shrimp are highest). Imitation crabmeat has less cholesterol, but more sodium, than real crabmeat.

- Choose water-packed tuna, salmon and sardines.

Oriental Barbecued Chicken (page 78),
Oriental Coleslaw (page 170),
Sole with Roasted Red Pepper Sauce (page 97)

Chicken Breasts with Sun-dried Tomato Sauce

4 SERVINGS (WITH ABOUT 1/3 CUP SAUCE EACH)

Be sure to purchase the dried tomatoes that are not packed in oil.

1/4 cup coarsely chopped sun-dried tomatoes (not oil-packed)

1/2 cup fat-free chicken broth

4 boneless, skinless chicken breast halves (about 1 pound)

1/2 cup sliced mushrooms (1 1/2 ounces)

2 tablespoons chopped green onions

2 cloves garlic, finely chopped

2 tablespoons dry red wine or fat-free chicken broth

1 teaspoon vegetable oil

1/2 cup skim milk

2 teaspoons cornstarch

2 teaspoons chopped fresh or 1/2 teaspoon dried basil leaves

2 cups hot cooked fettuccine

Mix tomatoes and broth. Let stand 30 minutes.

Trim fat from chicken. Cook mushrooms, onions and garlic in wine in 10-inch nonstick skillet over medium heat about 3 minutes, stirring occasionally, until mushrooms are tender; remove mixture from skillet.

Add oil to skillet. Cook chicken in oil over medium heat until brown on both sides. Add tomato mixture. Heat to boiling; reduce heat. Cover and simmer about 10 minutes, stirring occasionally, until juice of chicken is no longer pink when centers of thickest pieces are cut. Remove chicken pieces from skillet; keep warm.

Mix milk, cornstarch and basil; stir into tomato mixture. Heat to boiling, stirring constantly. Boil and stir 1 minute. Stir in mushroom mixture; heat through. Serve over chicken and fettuccine.

1 Serving:		% Daily Value:	
Calories	275	Vitamin A	2%
Calories from fat	55	Vitamin C	2%
Fat, g	6	Calcium	6%
Saturated, g	2	Iron	14%
Cholesterol, mg	90	**Diet Exchanges:**	
Sodium, mg	250	Starch/Bread	1
Carbohydrate, g	26	Lean meat	3
Dietary Fiber, g	2	Vegetable	2
Protein, g	31		

Chicken Breasts with Sun-dried Tomato Sauce

Oriental Barbecued Chicken

4 SERVINGS

⌛ 💧 ♥

Chicken thighs can be substituted for the breasts here, but they have about 9 milligrams more cholesterol per serving.

4 boneless, skinless chicken breast halves (about 1 pound)

1/2 cup hoisin sauce

1 tablespoon sesame oil

1 tablespoon tomato paste

1/2 teaspoon ground ginger

2 cloves garlic, finely chopped

Set oven control to broil. Spray broiler rack with nonstick cooking spray. Trim fat from chicken. Place chicken on rack in broiler pan. Mix remaining ingredients; brush on chicken.

Broil with tops about 4 inches from heat 7 to 8 minutes or until brown. Turn; brush with sauce. Broil 4 to 5 minutes longer or until juice of chicken is no longer pink when centers of thickest pieces are cut. Heat remaining sauce to boiling. Serve with chicken.

1 Serving:		% Daily Value:	
Calories	230	Vitamin A	6%
Calories from fat	70	Vitamin C	12%
Fat, g	8	Calcium	4%
Saturated, g	2	Iron	12%
Cholesterol, mg	60	**Diet Exchanges:**	
Sodium, mg	90	Starch/Bread	1
Carbohydrate, g	12	Lean meat	3
Dietary Fiber, g	1		
Protein, g	28		

Curried Chicken and Nectarines

4 SERVINGS (ABOUT 1 CUP EACH)

⌛ 💧 ♥

4 boneless, skinless chicken breast halves (about 1 pound)

2 tablespoons fat-free oil-and-vinegar dressing

1 teaspoon curry powder

1/4 cup raisins

1/4 cup sliced green onions (3 medium)

1/4 teaspoon salt

1 medium bell pepper, cut into 1/4-inch strips

2 small nectarines, cut into 1/4-inch slices

Hot cooked rice, if desired

Trim fat from chicken. Cut chicken crosswise into 1/2-inch strips. Mix dressing and curry powder in medium bowl. Add chicken; toss.

Heat 10-inch nonstick skillet over medium-high heat. Add chicken and remaining ingredients except nectarines and rice; stir-fry 4 to 6 minutes or until chicken is no longer pink in center. Carefully stir in nectarines; heat through. Serve with rice.

1 Serving:		% Daily Value:	
Calories	180	Vitamin A	2%
Calories from fat	25	Vitamin C	32%
Fat, g	3	Calcium	2%
Saturated, g	1	Iron	8%
Cholesterol, mg	60	**Diet Exchanges:**	
Sodium, mg	190	Lean meat	2
Carbohydrate, g	14	Fruit	1
Dietary Fiber, g	1		
Protein, g	25		

Spicy Cancún Drumsticks

4 SERVINGS (2 DRUMSTICKS EACH)

8 chicken drumsticks (about 1 3/4 pounds)

1/3 cup all-purpose flour

1/3 cup yellow cornmeal

1 teaspoon chopped fresh or 1/4 teaspoon dried oregano leaves

1 teaspoon chopped fresh or 1/4 teaspoon dried basil leaves

1/2 teaspoon ground cumin

1/2 teaspoon chili powder

1/4 teaspoon salt

1/8 teaspoon ground cloves

1/3 cup buttermilk

1/4 teaspoon red pepper sauce

Heat oven to 400°. Spray rectangular pan, 13 × 9 × 2 inches, with nonstick cooking spray. Remove skin and fat from chicken.

Mix remaining ingredients except buttermilk and pepper sauce in large plastic bag. Mix buttermilk and pepper sauce. Dip chicken into buttermilk, then shake in cornmeal mixture. Place in pan.

Spray chicken lightly with nonstick cooking spray. Bake uncovered 40 to 45 minutes or until juice is no longer pink when centers of thickest pieces are cut.

1 Serving:		% Daily Value:	
Calories	240	Vitamin A	2%
Calories from fat	55	Vitamin C	0%
Fat, g	6	Calcium	4%
Saturated, g	2	Iron	12%
Cholesterol, mg	70	**Diet Exchanges:**	
Sodium, mg	220	Starch/Bread	1
Carbohydrate, g	18	Lean meat	3
Dietary Fiber, g	1		
Protein, g	29		

Chicken and Grape Pilaf

4 SERVINGS (ABOUT 1 1/4 CUPS EACH)

A traditional pilaf calls for cooking rice in hot fat before cooking it in hot broth. This version eliminates that step for a lower-fat dish.

2 cups cubed cooked chicken or turkey

3/4 cup uncooked regular long grain rice

1/4 cup sliced green onions (3 medium)

1 3/4 cups fat-free chicken broth

1 teaspoon margarine or spread

1/4 teaspoon ground cinnamon

1/4 teaspoon ground allspice

1/8 teaspoon salt

1 cup seedless grape halves

2 tablespoons chopped pecans

Heat all ingredients except grape halves and pecans to boiling in 2-quart saucepan, stirring once or twice; reduce heat. Cover and simmer 14 minutes (do not lift cover or stir). Remove from heat.

Stir in grapes and pecans, fluffing rice lightly with fork. Cover and let steam 5 to 10 minutes.

1 Serving:		% Daily Value:	
Calories	330	Vitamin A	2%
Calories from fat	80	Vitamin C	4%
Fat, g	8	Calcium	4%
Saturated, g	2	Iron	16%
Cholesterol, mg	60	**Diet Exchanges:**	
Sodium, mg	480	Starch/Bread	1
Carbohydrate, g	37	Lean meat	3
Dietary Fiber, g	1	Vegetable	1
Protein, g	26	Fruit	1

Oven-fried Chicken Nuggets

6 SERVINGS (ABOUT 4 PIECES CHICKEN AND 3 TABLESPOONS SAUCE EACH)

Fast food without the fat! You won't believe these tasty morsels that are baked in a cornflake crumb crust. In addition to the two dipping sauces we suggest below, honey would be tasty too.

2 pounds boneless, skinless chicken breast halves or thighs

1 1/2 cups cornflakes

1/2 cup all-purpose flour

1/2 teaspoon paprika

3/4 teaspoon salt

1/2 teaspoon pepper

1/3 cup low-fat buttermilk

1/2 cup barbecue sauce

1/2 cup sweet-and-sour sauce

Heat oven to 400°. Line jelly roll pan, 15 1/2 × 10 1/2 × 1 inch, with aluminum foil. Trim fat from chicken. Cut chicken into 2-inch pieces. Place cornflakes, flour, paprika, salt and pepper in blender. Cover and blend on medium speed until cornflakes are reduced to crumbs; pour into bowl.

Place chicken and buttermilk in plastic bag with zipper top; seal and refrigerate 5 minutes, turning once. Dip chicken into cornflake mixture to coat. Place in pan. Spray chicken with nonstick cooking spray.

Bake about 30 minutes or until crisp and chicken is no longer pink in center. Serve with barbecue sauce and sweet-and-sour sauce.

1 Serving:		% Daily Value:	
Calories	280	Vitamin A	9%
Calories from fat	45	Vitamin C	5%
Fat, g	5	Calcium	5%
Saturated, g	1	Iron	18%
Cholesterol, mg	85	**Diet Exchanges:**	
Sodium, mg	666	Starch/Bread	2
Carbohydrate, g	24	Lean meat	3
Dietary Fiber, g	1		
Protein, g	35		

Oven-fried Chicken Nuggets

Southwest Chicken and Chili Stew

4 SERVINGS (ABOUT 1 1/4 CUPS EACH)

1 pound boneless, skinless chicken breast halves or thighs

2 1/4 cups fat-free chicken broth

4 cloves garlic, finely chopped

1 to 2 medium jalapeño chilies, seeded and diced

2 teaspoons all-purpose flour

1 medium red bell pepper, diced (1 cup)

1 medium carrot, sliced (1/2 cup)

1 cup whole kernel corn

1/4 teaspoon salt

1/4 teaspoon pepper

1/2 teaspoon ground cumin

2 tablespoons finely chopped fresh cilantro

1 teaspoon cornstarch

1/4 cup cold water

12 baked yellow, white or blue tortilla chips, coarsely crushed

Trim fat from chicken. Cut chicken into cubes. Heat 1/2 cup of the broth to boiling in Dutch oven. Cook chicken in broth about 5 minutes, stirring occasionally, until white. Remove chicken from broth with slotted spoon.

Cook garlic and chilies in broth in Dutch oven over medium-high heat 2 minutes, stirring frequently. Stir in flour. Cook over low heat 2 minutes, stirring constantly. Gradually stir in remaining broth.

Stir in chicken and remaining ingredients except cornstarch, water and tortilla chips. Heat to boiling heat; reduce heat. Cover and simmer about 20 minutes, stirring occasionally, until chicken is no longer pink in center.

Mix cornstarch and cold water; stir into stew. Cook, stirring frequently, until heated through and thickened. Serve sprinkled with tortilla chips.

1 Serving:		% Daily Value:	
Calories	225	Vitamin A	44%
Calories from fat	45	Vitamin C	52%
Fat, g	5	Calcium	4%
Saturated, g	1	Iron	12%
Cholesterol, mg	60	**Diet Exchanges:**	
Sodium, mg	810	Starch/Bread	1
Carbohydrate, g	18	Lean meat	2
Dietary Fiber, g	2	Vegetable	1
Protein, g	29		

Southwest Chicken and Chili Stew

Chicken-Vegetable Soup

4 SERVINGS (ABOUT 1 1/2 CUPS EACH)

This mildly flavored soup is chock-full of vegetables. There is no added salt called for because of the four cups of chicken broth. If your broth is low-salt, add salt to taste, if desired.

2 cups cubed cooked chicken or turkey

1 cup small cauliflowerets*

1 cup cut-up green beans*

4 cups fat-free chicken broth

1 teaspoon chopped fresh or 1/2 teaspoon dried tarragon leaves

1/8 teaspoon pepper

4 small new potatoes, cut into fourths

1 medium carrot, sliced (1/2 cup)

4 sprigs tarragon

Heat all ingredients to boiling; reduce heat. Cover and simmer 10 to 12 minutes, stirring occasionally, until vegetables are crisp-tender. Garnish each serving with tarragon sprig if desired.

*1 cup frozen cauliflower and 1 cup frozen cut green beans can be substituted for the fresh cauliflowerets and green beans (do not thaw).

1 Serving:		% Daily Value:	
Calories	260	Vitamin A	30%
Calories from fat	55	Vitamin C	22%
Fat, g	5	Calcium	6%
Saturated, g	2	Iron	18%
Cholesterol, mg	60	**Diet Exchanges:**	
Sodium, mg	860	Starch/Bread	1
Carbohydrate, g	27	Lean meat	2
Dietary Fiber, g	3	Vegetable	2
Protein, g	28		

Sesame Chicken Salad

4 SERVINGS (ABOUT 2 CUPS EACH)

3 cups uncooked farfalle (bow-tie) pasta (6 ounces)

1 1/2 cups cut-up cooked chicken

1 cup very thinly sliced carrots (1 1/2 medium)

1 cup shredded bok choy leaves

3/4 cup thinly sliced bok choy stems

1 tablespoon chopped seeded red chili

2 green onions, cut into 1/4-inch diagonal slices

Ginger Dressing (below)

Cook and drain pasta as directed on package. Rinse with cold water; drain. Toss pasta and remaining ingredients. Cover and refrigerate at least 2 hours.

GINGER DRESSING

1/4 cup lime juice

1/4 cup honey

1 tablespoon vegetable oil

2 teaspoons sesame seed, toasted

2 teaspoons reduced-sodium soy sauce

1 teaspoon finely chopped gingerroot or 1/2 teaspoon ground ginger

1 teaspoon sesame oil

Mix all ingredients.

1 Serving:		% Daily Value:	
Calories	395	Vitamin A	58%
Calories from fat	90	Vitamin C	22%
Fat, g	10	Calcium	6%
Saturated, g	2	Iron	18%
Cholesterol, mg	45	Diet Exchanges:	
Sodium, mg	180	Starch/Bread	3
Carbohydrate, g	57	Lean meat	2
Dietary Fiber, g	3	Vegetable	2
Protein, g	22		

Turkey with Cranberry Stuffing

4 SERVINGS (WITH ABOUT
2 TABLESPOONS SAUCE EACH)

The perfect lower-fat Thanksgiving dish for a small group or any meal. You won't miss all of the usual added butter in stuffing in the tart cranberry stuffing.

**2 turkey breast tenderloins
    (1 to 1 1/4 pounds)**

1/2 cup coarsely chopped cranberries

2 tablespoons packed brown sugar

1 1/2 cups soft bread cubes

2 tablespoons sliced green onions

1/2 teaspoon grated orange peel

2 tablespoons orange juice

1/4 teaspoon salt

1/4 teaspoon ground nutmeg

Nutmeg-Orange Sauce (right)

Heat oven to 400°. Spray square pan, $9 \times 9 \times 2$ inches, with nonstick cooking spray. Cut pocket lengthwise in each turkey breast tenderloin to within 1/2 inch of ends. Mix cranberries and brown sugar in medium bowl. Stir in remaining ingredients except Nutmeg-Orange Sauce. Spoon into pockets in turkey; secure with toothpicks. Place in pan.

Cover and bake 40 to 45 minutes or until juice of turkey is no longer pink when centers of thickest pieces are cut. Prepare Nutmeg-Orange Sauce. Serve with turkey.

NUTMEG-ORANGE SAUCE

1 tablespoon cornstarch

1/8 teaspoon ground nutmeg

Dash of salt

1 cup orange juice

Mix cornstarch, nutmeg and salt in 1 1/2-quart saucepan. Gradually stir in orange juice. Cook over medium heat, stirring constantly, until mixture thickens and boils. Boil and stir 1 minute.

1 Serving:		% Daily Value:	
Calories	245	Vitamin A	0%
Calories from fat	35	Vitamin C	24%
Fat, g	4	Calcium	4%
Saturated, g	1	Iron	10%
Cholesterol, mg	65	Diet Exchanges:	
Sodium, mg	330	Lean meat	2
Carbohydrate, g	25	Vegetable	1
Dietary Fiber, g	1	Fruit	1 1/2
Protein, g	28		

Turkey Cutlets with Marinara Sauce

4 SERVINGS (1 CUTLET AND 1/3 CUP SAUCE EACH)

1 pound turkey breast tenderloins

1 cup bread or cracker crumbs, toasted

1 teaspoon paprika

1 teaspoon dried thyme leaves

1 teaspoon ground mustard (dry)

1/2 teaspoon salt

3/4 cup fat-free chicken broth

3 medium onions, chopped (1 1/2 cups)

3/4 cup chopped celery

1 small red or yellow bell pepper, chopped (1/2 cup)

4 cloves garlic, finely chopped

1 cup chopped fresh or canned (drained) tomatoes

1 cup tomato juice

1/4 cup dry red wine or fat-free chicken broth

1 tablespoon tomato paste

1/2 teaspoon fennel seed

Heat oven to 400°. Line jelly roll pan, 15 1/2 × 10 1/2 × 1 inch, with aluminum foil. Cut each turkey tenderloin horizontally in half. Place in plastic bag with zipper top. Add bread crumbs, paprika, thyme, mustard and salt. Seal bag and turn to coat. Place turkey in pan. Spray turkey with nonstick cooking spray. Bake about 20 minutes or until no longer pink in center.

Heat broth to boiling in 3-quart saucepan over medium-high heat. Stir in onions, celery, bell pepper and garlic. Cook about 5 minutes, stirring frequently, until onion is tender. Stir in remaining ingredients. Heat to boiling; reduce heat to medium. Simmer uncovered 15 to 20 minutes, stirring occasionally, until sauce is thickened. Serve with turkey.

1 Serving:		% Daily Value:	
Calories	305	Vitamin A	18%
Calories from fat	55	Vitamin C	42%
Fat, g	6	Calcium	12%
Saturated, g	2	Iron	24%
Cholesterol, mg	70	**Diet Exchanges:**	
Sodium, mg	990	Starch/Bread	2
Carbohydrate, g	34	Lean meat	2
Dietary Fiber, g	4	Vegetable	1
Protein, g	33		

Turkey Cutlets with Marinara Sauce

Turkey-Broccoli Stir-fry

4 SERVINGS (1 CUP TURKEY MIXTURE AND
1 CUP RICE EACH)

1/2 pound turkey breast tenderloin, cubed

2 tablespoons soy sauce

1 teaspoon cornstarch

1 teaspoon sugar

3/4 cup fat-free chicken broth

2 tablespoons grated gingerroot

2 cloves garlic, finely chopped

1 teaspoon dark sesame oil

1 medium onion, chopped (1/2 cup)

1 small red bell pepper, sliced (1/2 cup)

3 cups broccoli flowerets

1 tablespoon hoisin sauce

4 cups cooked hot rice

Mix turkey, soy sauce, cornstarch, sugar and 1/4 cup of the broth. Cover and refrigerate 15 minutes.

Remove turkey from marinade; reserve marinade. Heat 1/4 cup of the broth to boiling in nonstick wok or 10-inch skillet. Add gingerroot and garlic; stir-fry 1 minute. Add oil, remaining 1/4 cup broth, the turkey, onion and bell pepper to wok; stir-fry 3 to 4 minutes or until turkey is white. Stir in broccoli. Cover and cook 2 to 3 minutes or until broccoli is crisp-tender and turkey is no longer pink in center. Stir in hoisin sauce and marinade. Heat to boiling; cook, stirring constantly, until thickened. Serve over rice.

1 Serving:		% Daily Value:	
Calories	330	Vitamin A	14%
Calories from fat	35	Vitamin C	64%
Fat, g	4	Calcium	6%
Saturated, g	1	Iron	18%
Cholesterol, mg	35	**Diet Exchanges:**	
Sodium, mg	710	Starch/Bread	3
Carbohydrate, g	55	Lean meat	1
Dietary Fiber, g	3	Vegetable	2
Protein, g	21		

Soft Turkey Tacos with Spicy Sauce

4 SERVINGS (2 TORTILLAS WITH
1 CUP FILLING EACH)

Fusion food at its best, tacos aren't just for ground beef and packaged taco seasoning anymore!

8 fat-free flour tortillas (7 to 8 inches in diameter)

1/2 cup fat-free chicken broth

1 medium onion, chopped (1/2 cup)

1 small red or green bell pepper, diced (1/2 cup)

1/2 cup whole kernel corn

1/2 pound lean ground turkey

4 cloves garlic, finely chopped

3 tablespoons Asian fish sauce or soy sauce

1 large jalapeño chili, finely chopped (2 tablespoons)

1/4 cup packed brown sugar

1/4 cup chopped fresh cilantro

Heat oven to 300°. Wrap tortillas in aluminum foil. Heat in oven 15 minutes.

Heat broth to boiling in nonstick wok or 10-inch skillet. Add onion, bell pepper and corn; stir-fry 2 to 3 minutes or until vegetables are crisp-tender. Add turkey and garlic; stir-fry 2 minutes.

Mix fish sauce, chili and brown sugar; stir into turkey mixture. Cook 3 to 5 minutes or until liquid is evaporated. Stir in cilantro. Spoon scant 1/2 cup turkey mixture onto center of each tortilla; roll up tortilla.

1 Serving:		% Daily Value:	
Calories	400	Vitamin A	20%
Calories from fat	55	Vitamin C	40%
Fat, g	6	Calcium	14%
Saturated, g	1	Iron	26%
Cholesterol, mg	40	**Diet Exchanges:**	
Sodium, mg	1,380	Starch/Bread	4
Carbohydrate, g	70	Lean meat	1/2
Dietary Fiber, g	3	Vegetable	2
Protein, g	19		

Turkey Pot Pie

4 SERVINGS

1 tablespoon margarine or spread

1 small onion, chopped (1/4 cup)

1 1/4 cups fat-free chicken broth

2 tablespoons cornstarch

1/2 cup skim milk

1 teaspoon chopped fresh or 1/4 teaspoon dried rosemary leaves, crumbled

2 cups cut-up cooked turkey breast

1 package (10 ounces) frozen peas and carrots

Biscuit Crust (right)

Heat oven to 425°. Melt margarine in 2-quart saucepan over medium-high heat. Cook onion in margarine, stirring frequently, until crisp-tender; reduce heat to medium. Mix 1/4 cup of the broth and the cornstarch. Stir cornstarch mixture, remaining 1 cup broth, the milk and rosemary into onion mixture. Heat to boiling, stirring constantly. Boil and stir 1 minute.

Stir in turkey and frozen peas and carrots, breaking up peas and carrots if necessary. Pour into ungreased square pan, 8 × 8 × 2 inches.

Prepare Biscuit Crust; place on turkey mixture. Bake about 30 minutes or until bubbly and crust is golden brown.

BISCUIT CRUST

1 tablespoon firm margarine or spread

1 cup all-purpose flour

1 1/4 teaspoons baking powder

1/8 teaspoon salt

1/3 cup low-fat sour cream

3 tablespoons skim milk

Cut margarine into flour, baking powder and salt in medium bowl, using pastry blender or criss-crossing 2 knives, until mixture looks like fine crumbs. Mix sour cream and milk until smooth. Stir sour cream mixture into flour mixture until dough leaves side of bowl. Turn dough onto lightly floured surface. Knead lightly 10 times. Pat into 8-inch square. Cut into four 4-inch squares.

1 Square:		% Daily Value:	
Calories	350	Vitamin A	68%
Calories from fat	81	Vitamin C	4%
Fat, g	9	Calcium	20%
Saturated, g	3	Iron	20%
Cholesterol, mg	55	**Diet Exchanges:**	
Sodium, mg	680	Starch/Bread	2
Carbohydrate, g	41	Lean meat	2
Dietary Fiber, g	4	Vegetable	2
Protein, g	30		

Turkey Meatballs with Corkscrew Pasta

4 SERVINGS (ABOUT 3 MEATBALLS AND 1/2 CUP SAUCE OVER 1 CUP PASTA EACH)

1/2 pound lean ground turkey

1/3 cup soft bread crumbs (1/2 slice bread)

1/3 cup finely chopped onion

1 tablespoon Worcestershire sauce

1/8 teaspoon ground red pepper (cayenne)

2 cloves garlic, finely chopped

2/3 cup raisins

1/4 cup finely chopped fresh parsley

1/4 cup tomato paste

2/3 cup fat-free chicken broth

2 tablespoons sugar

2 tablespoons chopped fresh or 2 teaspoons dried basil leaves

2 teaspoons chopped fresh or 1 teaspoon dried oregano leaves

1 teaspoon salt

2 cans (16 ounces each) whole tomatoes, undrained

4 cups hot cooked rotelle (corkscrew) pasta

Spray 10-inch nonstick skillet with nonstick cooking spray. Mix turkey, bread crumbs, onion, Worcestershire sauce, red pepper and garlic. Shape mixture into 1-inch balls. Cook meatballs in skillet over medium-high heat until brown on all sides.

Stir in remaining ingredients except pasta, breaking up tomatoes. Heat to boiling; reduce heat to low. Cook about 15 minutes or until meatballs are no longer pink in center. Serve over pasta.

1 Serving:		% Daily Value:	
Calories	495	Vitamin A	22%
Calories from fat	70	Vitamin C	40%
Fat, g	8	Calcium	14%
Saturated, g	2	Iron	36%
Cholesterol, mg	40	**Diet Exchanges:**	
Sodium, mg	1,320	Starch/Bread	4
Carbohydrate, g	88	Medium-fat meat	1
Dietary Fiber, g	6	Vegetable	2
Protein, g	24	Fruit	1

Turkey Meatballs with Corkscrew Pasta

Poaching for Less Fat, More Flavor

Poaching is a low-fat cooking method that uses liquids and seasonings to infuse a subtle flavor into the food being poached. Water can certainly be used but other liquids like wine, broth and fruit juices will add more flavor. In addition to chicken breasts and fish, which we include here, fruits and eggs are other foods that are often poached.

POACHED CHICKEN BREASTS

4 SERVINGS

Trim fat from 4 boneless, skinless chicken breast halves (about 1 pound). Place chicken, 1/4 cup water, 1 tablespoon lemon juice and 1/4 teaspoon salt in 10-inch nonstick skillet. Heat to boiling; reduce heat. Cover and simmer about 10 minutes or until juice of chicken is no longer pink when centers of thickest pieces are cut.

Remove chicken from skillet with slotted spatula; drain. Serve immediately, or cover and refrigerate up to 2 days for cold dishes.

1 Serving:		% Daily Value:	
Calories	125	Vitamin A	0%
Calories from fat	25	Vitamin C	0%
Fat, g	3	Calcium	0%
Saturated, g	1	Iron	4%
Cholesterol, mg	60	**Diet Exchanges:**	
Sodium, mg	190	Lean meat	2
Carbohydrate, g	0		
Dietary Fiber, g	0		
Protein, g	24		

POACHED FISH FILLETS

4 SERVINGS

Place 1 pound firm lean fish fillets (see chart on page 212), cut into 4 serving pieces, 2 cups water, 1/3 cup low-fat milk, 1/4 teaspoon salt and 1 lemon, thinly sliced, in 10-inch nonstick skillet. Heat to boiling; reduce heat. Simmer uncovered 8 to 10 minutes or until fish flakes easily with fork.

Remove fillets from skillet with slotted spatula; drain. Serve immediately, or cover and refrigerate up to 2 days for cold dishes.

1 Serving:		% Daily Value:	
Calories	100	Vitamin A	0%
Calories from fat	20	Vitamin C	0%
Fat, g	2	Calcium	2%
Saturated, g	0	Iron	2%
Cholesterol, mg	60	**Diet Exchanges:**	
Sodium, mg	170	Lean meat	2
Carbohydrate, g	0		
Dietary Fiber, g	0		
Protein, g	21		

OVEN-POACHED FISH STEAKS

4 SERVINGS

Heat oven to 450°. Place 4 lean fish steaks (see chart on page 212), 1 inch thick (about 1 1/2 pounds), in ungreased rectangular baking dish, 11 × 7 × 1 1/2 inches. Sprinkle with 1/4 teaspoon salt and 1/8 teaspoon pepper. Place 1 sprig of dill weed and 1 slice of lemon on each steak. Pour 1/4 cup dry white wine or water over fish. Bake uncovered 20 to 25 minutes or until fish flakes easily with fork.

Remove steaks from dish with slotted spatula; drain. Serve immediately, or cover and refrigerate up to 2 days for cold dishes.

1 Serving:		% Daily Value:	
Calories	145	Vitamin A	0%
Calories from fat	20	Vitamin C	0%
Fat, g	2	Calcium	2%
Saturated, g	0	Iron	2%
Cholesterol, mg	90	**Diet Exchanges:**	
Sodium, mg	270	Lean meat	3
Carbohydrate, g	0		
Dietary Fiber, g	0		
Protein, g	32		

Salmon with Dilled Cucumbers

4 SERVINGS (WITH ABOUT 1/4 CUP CUCUMBERS EACH)

**4 salmon or halibut steaks, 3/4 inch thick
(about 1 1/2 pounds)**

**1 tablespoon chopped fresh or 1/2 teaspoon
dried dill weed**

1/4 teaspoon salt

1/4 cup water

1 tablespoon lemon juice

Dilled Cucumbers (right)

Place fish in 10-inch nonstick skillet. Sprinkle with
dill weed and salt. Pour water and lemon juice into
skillet. Heat to boiling; reduce heat. Cover and
cook 15 to 20 minutes or until fish flakes easily
with fork. Meanwhile, prepare Dilled Cucumbers.
Serve over fish.

DILLED CUCUMBERS

1 medium cucumber

**1 tablespoon chopped fresh or 1 teaspoon
dried dill weed**

1 tablespoon white vinegar

1 1/2 teaspoons sugar

1/4 teaspoon salt

Peel cucumber. Cut lengthwise in half; seed and
cut into thin slices. Mix cucumber and remaining
ingredients in 1 1/2-quart saucepan. Cook over
high heat 1 to 2 minutes, stirring frequently, until
cucumber is crisp-tender.

1 Serving:		% Daily Value:	
Calories	245	Vitamin A	6%
Calories from fat	90	Vitamin C	4%
Fat, g	10	Calcium	2%
Saturated, g	3	Iron	6%
Cholesterol, mg	110	**Diet Exchanges:**	
Sodium, mg	300	Lean meat	4
Carbohydrate, g	3	Vegetable	1
Dietary Fiber, g	0		
Protein, g	36		

*Salmon with Dilled Cucumbers, Warm Greens with Balsamic
Vinaigrette (page 175)*

Baked Flounder Teriyaki

4 SERVINGS

6 small flounder or other lean fish fillets (about 1 1/2 pounds)

1/3 cup dry sherry or apple juice

2 tablespoons chopped green onions

3 tablespoons lemon juice

2 teaspoons finely chopped gingerroot

2 teaspoons honey

1 teaspoon vegetable oil

1/4 teaspoon pepper

2 cloves garlic, finely chopped

Spray rectangular pan, 13 × 9 × 2 inches, with nonstick cooking spray. Place fish in pan. Mix remaining ingredients; spoon over fish. Cover with aluminum foil and refrigerate 1 hour.

Heat oven to 375°. Bake covered 15 to 20 minutes or until fish flakes easily with fork.

1 Serving:		% Daily Value:	
Calories	105	Vitamin A	0%
Calories from fat	20	Vitamin C	0%
Fat, g	2	Calcium	2%
Saturated, g	0	Iron	2%
Cholesterol, mg	55	**Diet Exchanges:**	
Sodium, mg	85	Lean meat	2
Carbohydrate, g	2		
Dietary Fiber, g	0		
Protein, g	20		

Tropical Mahimahi

4 SERVINGS (WITH 1/4 CUP SALSA EACH)

The fresh flavors of citrus and pineapple titillate the taste buds in this tropical dish from the deep blue sea. And you thought fish was only good when swimming in butter!

1 pound mahimahi or other lean fish steaks, 3/4 inch thick

1/3 cup orange juice

3 tablespoons lime juice

2 tablespoons honey

1/4 teaspoon salt

1 clove garlic, finely chopped

1 cup Pineapple Salsa (page 179)

Cut fish into 4 serving pieces. Place in ungreased square baking dish, 8 × 8 × 2 inches. Mix remaining ingredients except Pineapple Salsa; pour over fish. Cover and refrigerate at least 1 hour but no longer than 6 hours, turning once.

Set oven control to broil. Spray broiler pan rack with nonstick cooking spray. Remove fish from marinade; reserve marinade. Place fish on rack in broiler pan. Broil with tops about 4 inches from heat 12 to 15 minutes, turning and brushing with marinade after 6 minutes, until fish flakes easily with fork. Discard any remaining marinade. Serve fish with Pineapple Salsa.

1 Serving:		% Daily Value:	
Calories	180	Vitamin A	18%
Calories from fat	20	Vitamin C	46%
Fat, g	2	Calcium	2%
Saturated, g	0	Iron	4%
Cholesterol, mg	60	**Diet Exchanges:**	
Sodium, mg	240	Lean meat	2
Carbohydrate, g	18	Fruit	1
Dietary Fiber, g	1		
Protein, g	23		

Sole with Roasted Red Pepper Sauce

4 SERVINGS (WITH ABOUT 1/4 CUP SAUCE EACH)

Both bell peppers and jalapeño chilies can be roasted under the broiler or over a range-top flame. Due to their difference in size, it's not efficient to roast them together under the broiler. Brown the jalapeños over a burner while the bells broil, then toss them into the plastic bag together. Always use care when handling hot chilies; rubber gloves are recommended.

2 medium red bell peppers*

1 jalapeño chili

1/3 cup reduced-fat sour cream

1/2 teaspoon sugar

1 pound sole or other lean fish fillets

4 cups bite-size pieces salad greens

Set oven control to broil. Place bell peppers on rack in broiler pan. Broil with tops about 5 inches from heat 12 to 16 minutes, turning occasionally, until skin is blistered and evenly browned. Place peppers in plastic bag; close tightly. Let stand 15 to 20 minutes. Peel peppers; remove stem, seeds and membranes.

Hold chili over stove-top burner, using long-handled fork. Turn frequently until skin is blistered and evenly browned. Place chili in plastic bag; close tightly. Let stand 15 to 20 minutes. Peel chili; remove stem, seeds and membranes.

Place peppers and chili in blender or food processor. Cover and blend until smooth. Mix pepper mixture, sour cream and sugar.

Set oven control to broil. Spray broiler rack with nonstick cooking spray. Cut fish into 4 serving pieces. Place on rack in broiler pan. Broil with tops about 4 inches from heat 5 to 6 minutes or until fish flakes easily with fork (do not turn). Place salad greens on 4 serving plates. Top each with fish. Serve with sauce.

*One 7.25-ounce jar of roasted red peppers, drained, can be used instead of roasting your own bell peppers.

1 Serving:		% Daily Value:	
Calories	140	Vitamin A	38%
Calories from fat	25	Vitamin C	78%
Fat, g	3	Calcium	6%
Saturated, g	1	Iron	4%
Cholesterol, mg	60	**Diet Exchanges:**	
Sodium, mg	110	Lean meat	2
Carbohydrate, g	8	Vegetable	1
Dietary Fiber, g	1		
Protein, g	21		

Caribbean Fish Salad

4 SERVINGS (1 1/2 CUPS EACH)

Spraying the fish with nonstick cooking spray before broiling is a technique to make the small amount of oil in the spray go a long way toward keeping the fish moist while broiling.

4 ounces Chinese pea pods

1 large salmon fillet (about 1 pound)

4 cups bite-size pieces leaf lettuce or spinach

1 cup thinly sliced red bell pepper

1/4 cup finely chopped fresh parsley

1/4 cup plain fat-free yogurt

2 tablespoons lime juice

1 tablespoon frozen (thawed) orange juice concentrate

1 tablespoon olive or vegetable oil

1/2 teaspoon salt

1 large papaya, seeded and diced (2 cups)

Remove strings from pea pods. Place pea pods in boiling water; heat to boiling. Immediately rinse in cold water; drain. Cut pea pods into julienne strips.

Set oven control to broil. Spray salmon with nonstick cooking spray; place on rack in broiler pan. Broil with top about 4 inches from heat about 5 minutes or until fish flakes easily with fork (do not turn); cool slightly. Separate into large flakes with fork. Place fish, pea pods and remaining ingredients in large bowl; toss.

1 Serving:		% Daily Value:	
Calories	250	Vitamin A	30%
Calories from fat	90	Vitamin C	100%
Fat, g	10	Calcium	10%
Saturated, g	2	Iron	12%
Cholesterol, mg	75	**Diet Exchanges:**	
Sodium, mg	360	Starch/Bread	1/2
Carbohydrate, g	17	Lean meat	3
Dietary Fiber, g	4	Vegetable	2
Protein, g	27		

Caribbean Fish Salad

Parmesan-Basil Perch

4 SERVINGS

1 pound ocean perch or other lean fish fillets

2 tablespoons dry bread crumbs

1 tablespoon grated reduced-fat Parmesan cheese blend

1 tablespoon chopped fresh or 1 teaspoon dried basil leaves

1/2 teaspoon paprika

Dash of pepper

1 tablespoon margarine or spread, melted

2 tablespoons chopped fresh parsley

Move oven rack to position slightly above middle of oven. Heat oven to 500°. Spray rectangular pan, 13 × 9 × 2 inches, with nonstick cooking spray. Cut fish into 4 serving pieces. Mix remaining ingredients except margarine and parsley. Brush one side of fish with margarine; dip into crumb mixture. Place fish, coated sides up, in pan.

Bake uncovered about 10 minutes or until fish flakes easily with fork. Sprinkle with parsley.

1 Serving:		% Daily Value:	
Calories	145	Vitamin A	8%
Calories from fat	45	Vitamin C	2%
Fat, g	5	Calcium	4%
Saturated, g	1	Iron	4%
Cholesterol, mg	60	**Diet Exchanges:**	
Sodium, mg	180	Lean meat	2
Carbohydrate, g	3	Vegetable	1
Dietary Fiber, g	0		
Protein, g	22		

Tuna with Pear Salsa

6 SERVINGS (WITH ABOUT 1/4 CUP SALSA EACH)

Pear Salsa (below)

6 small yellowfin tuna or other lean fish fillets (about 1 1/2 pounds)

Prepare Pear Salsa. Set oven control to broil. Spray broiler pan rack with nonstick cooking spray. Place fish on rack in broiler pan. Broil with tops about 4 inches from heat about 5 minutes or until fish flakes easily with fork (do not turn). Top with salsa.

PEAR SALSA

1 large unpeeled pear, chopped (1 1/2 cups)

2 tablespoons chopped green onions

2 tablespoons chopped fresh cilantro

1 medium hot yellow chili, chopped (2 tablespoons)

2 teaspoons grated lemon peel

2 tablespoons lemon juice

1/2 teaspoon salt

Mix all ingredients in glass or plastic bowl. Cover and refrigerate 1 hour.

1 Serving:		% Daily Value:	
Calories	130	Vitamin A	4%
Calories from fat	20	Vitamin C	8%
Fat, g	2	Calcium	2%
Saturated, g	0	Iron	2%
Cholesterol, mg	60	**Diet Exchanges:**	
Sodium, mg	280	Lean meat	2
Carbohydrate, g	7	Fruit	1/2
Dietary Fiber, g	1		
Protein, g	22		

Creamy Pasta with Broiled Tuna

4 SERVINGS (1 1/2 CUPS EACH)

1 1/2 teaspoons soy sauce

1 teaspoon dark sesame oil

2 cloves garlic, finely chopped

1 pound tuna steak (about 1 large)

2 cups uncooked medium pasta shells
   (5 ounces)

1/2 cup fat-free chicken broth

2 tablespoons all-purpose flour

1 1/3 cups skim milk

2 tablespoons reduced-fat sour cream

1/8 teaspoon ground nutmeg

1 cup fresh or frozen green peas

2 tablespoons chopped fresh parsley

1/4 teaspoon salt

1/8 teaspoon pepper

Mix soy sauce, oil and garlic in shallow glass or plastic dish. Add tuna; turn to coat. Cover and refrigerate 20 minutes. Cook and drain pasta as directed on package.

Set oven control to broil. Spray broiler pan rack with nonstick cooking spray. Remove tuna from marinade; reserve marinade. Place tuna on rack in broiler pan. Broil with top 4 inches from heat about 7 minutes, turning after 3 minutes and brushing with marinade, until fish flakes easily with fork; cool slightly. Separate tuna into large flakes with fork.

Heat broth to boiling in 10-inch nonstick skillet over medium-high heat. Stir in flour. Cook 2 minutes, stirring constantly. Stir in milk, sour cream, nutmeg and peas; reduce heat. Simmer uncovered 3 minutes, stirring frequently, until slightly thickened. Stir in parsley, salt, pepper, pasta and tuna; heat through.

1 Serving:		% Daily Value:	
Calories	440	Vitamin A	78%
Calories from fat	80	Vitamin C	6%
Fat, g	9	Calcium	14%
Saturated, g	2	Iron	22%
Cholesterol, mg	45	**Diet Exchanges:**	
Sodium, mg	490	Starch/Bread	3
Carbohydrate, g	54	Lean meat	2
Dietary Fiber, g	3	Vegetable	1
Protein, g	39	Skim milk	1/2

Savory Fish en Papillote

4 SERVINGS

⧗ ◊ ♡

1 pound orange roughy or other lean fish fillets

4 twelve-inch circles cooking parchment paper

4 teaspoons chopped fresh or 1 teaspoon dried oregano leaves

1/4 teaspoon salt

1/8 teaspoon pepper

1 small onion, thinly sliced

1 small tomato, thinly sliced

1 small zucchini, thinly sliced

1/4 cup sliced ripe olives

Heat oven to 400°. Cut fish into 4 serving pieces. Place each piece fish on half of each parchment circle. Sprinkle fish with oregano, salt and pepper. Layer onion, tomato, zucchini and olives on fish. Fold other half of circle over fish and vegetables. Beginning at one end, seal edge by turning up and folding tightly 2 or 3 times. Twist each end several times to secure. Place on ungreased cookie sheet.

Bake 20 to 25 minutes or until vegetables are crisp-tender and fish flakes easily with fork. To serve, cut a large X in top of each packet; fold back points.

1 Serving:		% Daily Value:	
Calories	120	Vitamin A	4%
Calories from fat	20	Vitamin C	6%
Fat, g	2	Calcium	4%
Saturated, g	0	Iron	4%
Cholesterol, mg	60	**Diet Exchanges:**	
Sodium, mg	310	Lean meat	2
Carbohydrate, g	4	Vegetable	1
Dietary Fiber, g	1		
Protein, g	23		

Fish Burritos

4 SERVINGS

⧗ ◊ ♡

Definitely not the traditional burrito. The availability of fat-free tortillas makes this dish even more inviting.

4 fat-free flour tortillas (8 inches in diameter)

1 pound scrod or other lean fish fillets

1/3 cup yellow cornmeal

1/2 teaspoon salt

1 tablespoon vegetable oil

1/2 cup green sauce

Heat oven to 300°. Wrap tortillas in aluminum foil. Heat in oven 15 minutes. Cut fish into 1-inch pieces. Mix cornmeal and salt in small bowl. Coat fish with cornmeal mixture; shake off excess.

Heat oil in 10-inch nonstick skillet over medium-high heat. Cook fish in oil 6 to 7 minutes, turning occasionally, until fish flakes easily with fork. Divide fish among tortillas. Top each with 2 tablespoons green sauce; roll up tortilla.

1 Serving:		% Daily Value:	
Calories	280	Vitamin A	18%
Calories from fat	45	Vitamin C	8%
Fat, g	5	Calcium	8%
Saturated, g	1	Iron	12%
Cholesterol, mg	60	**Diet Exchanges:**	
Sodium, mg	770	Starch/Bread	2
Carbohydrate, g	34	Lean meat	2
Dietary Fiber, g	2	Vegetable	1
Protein, g	27		

Broiled Caribbean Swordfish

4 SERVINGS (WITH ABOUT 1/2 CUP SALSA EACH)

4 swordfish or shark steaks, 1 inch thick (about 1 1/2 pounds)

1 tablespoon grated lime peel

1/4 cup lime juice

1/4 cup grapefruit juice

1/2 teaspoon salt

1 clove garlic, finely chopped

Papaya Salsa (right)

Place fish in ungreased square baking dish, 8 × 8 × 2 inches. Mix lime peel, fruit juices, salt and garlic; pour over fish. Cover and refrigerate 2 hours. Prepare Papaya Salsa.

Set oven control to broil. Spray broiler pan rack with nonstick cooking spray. Remove fish from marinade; reserve marinade. Place fish on rack in broiler pan. Broil with tops about 4 inches from heat about 16 minutes, turning and brushing with marinade after 8 minutes, until fish flakes easily with fork. Serve fish with salsa.

PAPAYA SALSA

1 large papaya, peeled, seeded and chopped (2 cups)

1/4 cup finely chopped red bell pepper

1 tablespoon finely chopped green onion

1 tablespoon chopped fresh cilantro

2 to 3 tablespoons grapefruit juice

1/8 teaspoon salt

Mix all ingredients in glass or plastic bowl. Cover and refrigerate 1 hour.

1 Serving:		% Daily Value:	
Calories	230	Vitamin A	10%
Calories from fat	70	Vitamin C	66%
Fat, g	8	Calcium	4%
Saturated, g	2	Iron	6%
Cholesterol, mg	90	**Diet Exchanges:**	
Sodium, mg	280	Lean meat	3
Carbohydrate, g	12	Vegetable	1
Dietary Fiber, g	2	Fruit	1/2
Protein, g	29		

Seafood Stew with Rosamarina

12 mussels, scrubbed and debearded

8 uncooked medium shrimp in shells

1 teaspoon vegetable oil

1/2 cup chopped green onions (8 medium)

1 clove garlic, finely chopped

1 large tomato, coarsely chopped (1 cup)

1 medium carrot, thinly sliced (1/2 cup)

1/3 cup uncooked rosamarina (orzo) pasta

1 can (14 1/2 ounces) reduced-sodium chicken broth

1 bottle (8 ounces) clam juice

1/2 cup dry white wine or reduced-sodium chicken broth

1 tablespoon chopped fresh or 1 teaspoon dried thyme leaves

2 teaspoons chopped fresh or 1/2 teaspoon dried dill weed

6 drops red pepper sauce

1/2 pound red snapper fillets, skinned and cut into 1/2-inch pieces

1/2 cup sliced mushrooms (1 1/2 ounces)

Chopped fresh parsley, if desired

Lemon wedges, if desired

Discard any mussels that are broken or open (dead). Peel shrimp. Make a shallow cut lengthwise down back of each shrimp; wash out vein.

Heat oil in nonstick Dutch oven over medium heat. Cook onions and garlic in oil about 5 minutes, stirring occasionally., until onions are tender. Stir in tomato, carrot, pasta, broth, clam juice, wine, thyme, dill weed and pepper sauce. Heat to boiling; reduce heat. Cover and simmer about 20 minutes, stirring occasionally, until pasta is almost tender.

Stir in mussels, shrimp, fish and mushrooms. Cover and heat to boiling; reduce heat. Simmer 6 to 8 minutes, stirring occasionally, until fish flakes easily with fork and mussels open (discard any unopened mussels). Sprinkle with parsley. Serve with lemon wedges. 4 servings (about 1 1/2 cups each).

1 Serving:		% Daily Value:	
Calories	180	Vitamin A	36%
Calories from fat	25	Vitamin C	16%
Fat, g	3	Calcium	6%
Saturated, g	1	Iron	48%
Cholesterol, mg	65	**Diet Exchanges:**	
Sodium, mg	410	Starch/Bread	1
Carbohydrate, g	16	Lean meat	2
Dietary Fiber, g	1		
Protein, g	23		

Seafood Stew with Rosamarina

Thai Shrimp and Rice Noodle Nests

4 SERVINGS (1/2 CUP SHRIMP MIXTURE AND 1 CUP NOODLES EACH)

Look for canned coconut milk marked "lite" when looking for reduced-fat coconut milk. Leftover milk can be frozen in small quantities for future uses.

1/4 cup finely chopped fresh basil leaves

1/4 cup Asian fish sauce or soy sauce

1/4 cup lime juice

2 tablespoons packed brown sugar

1 tablespoon cornstarch

1 pound uncooked peeled deveined medium shrimp, cut into pieces

2/3 cup fat-free chicken broth

6 cloves garlic, finely chopped

1 jalapeño chili, finely chopped

1 cup julienned broccoli stems or flowerets

2/3 cup shredded carrot (1 medium)

2/3 cup finely chopped red or green bell pepper

1/4 cup chopped fresh cilantro

3 tablespoons reduced-fat coconut milk

4 cups hot cooked rice noodles or linguine

Mix basil, fish sauce, lime juice, brown sugar and cornstarch in shallow glass or plastic dish. Stir in shrimp. Cover and refrigerate 20 minutes.

Heat broth to boiling in nonstick wok or 10-inch skillet. Add garlic, chili and broccoli; stir-fry 5 to 8 minutes or until broccoli is crisp-tender. Add carrot and bell pepper; stir-fry 3 minutes. Add shrimp and marinade; stir-fry 3 to 5 minutes or until shrimp are pink and sauce thickens slightly. Stir in cilantro and coconut milk; remove from heat.

Coil 1 cup noodles in center of each plate. Top with 1/2 cup shrimp mixture.

1 Serving:		% Daily Value:	
Calories	305	Vitamin A	58%
Calories from fat	25	Vitamin C	68%
Fat, g	3	Calcium	8%
Saturated, g	2	Iron	28%
Cholesterol, mg	160	**Diet Exchanges:**	
Sodium, mg	1,370	Starch/Bread	3
Carbohydrate, g	50	Lean meat	1
Dietary Fiber, g	2	Vegetable	1
Protein, g	22		

Thai Shrimp and Rice Noodle Nest

Quick Jambalaya

4 SERVINGS

▧ ◖ ♡

2 teaspoons margarine or spread

1 large onion, chopped (1 cup)

1 medium stalk celery, chopped (1/2 cup)

1 small green bell pepper, chopped (1/2 cup)

2 cloves garlic, finely chopped

1 cup uncooked peeled deveined small
   shrimp (1/2 pound)

1/2 cup fat-free chicken broth

1/2 teaspoon dried basil leaves

1/2 teaspoon dried thyme leaves

1/4 teaspoon pepper

1/8 teaspoon red pepper sauce

1 bay leaf

1 can (14 1/2 ounces) peeled diced
   tomatoes, undrained

3 cups cooked quick-cooking brown or
   instant rice

Melt margarine in 3-quart saucepan over medium-high heat. Cook onion, celery, bell pepper and garlic in margarine, stirring frequently, until onion is tender. Stir in remaining ingredients except rice. Heat to boiling; reduce heat. Cover and simmer 5 minutes. Stir in rice. Cover and let stand 10 minutes. Remove bay leaf.

1 Serving:		% Daily Value:	
Calories	245	Vitamin A	12%
Calories from fat	35	Vitamin C	26%
Fat, g	4	Calcium	8%
Saturated, g	1	Iron	14%
Cholesterol, mg	60	**Diet Exchanges:**	
Sodium, mg	380	Starch/Bread	2 1/2
Carbohydrate, g	44	Vegetable	1
Dietary Fiber, g	5		
Protein, g	13		

Shellfish Pasta Gumbo

6 SERVINGS (1 1/4 CUPS EACH)

▧ ◖

1 tablespoon olive or vegetable oil

1/4 cup dry white wine or fat-free chicken
   broth

3 medium onions, chopped (1 1/2 cups)

1 medium green bell pepper, chopped
   (1 cup)

6 cloves garlic, finely chopped

1 teaspoon cornstarch

1 tablespoon cold water

3 cups chopped fresh or canned (drained)
   tomatoes

1/3 cup chopped fresh or frozen okra
   (3 medium)

1 teaspoon chopped fresh or 1/2 teaspoon
   dried thyme leaves

1/2 teaspoon salt

1/2 teaspoon crushed red pepper

1/2 pound uncooked peeled deveined
   medium shrimp

1/2 pound bay scallops

3 cups cooked pasta

Heat oil and wine in Dutch oven over medium-high heat. Cook onions, bell pepper and garlic in wine mixture 8 to 10 minutes, stirring frequently, until vegetables are tender.

Stir in tomatoes, okra, thyme, salt and red pepper. Cook 10 minutes, stirring occasionally. Stir in shrimp, scallops and pasta. Cook 3 to 5 minutes, stirring occasionally, until shrimp are pink and scallops are white. Mix cornstarch and water; stir in to shrimp mixture. Cook and stir 1 minute.

1 Serving:		% Daily Value:	
Calories	230	Vitamin A	10%
Calories from fat	35	Vitamin C	30%
Fat, g	4	Calcium	8%
Saturated, g	1	Iron	20%
Cholesterol, mg	65	**Diet Exchanges:**	
Sodium, mg	350	Starch/Bread	2
Carbohydrate, g	32	Lean meat	1
Dietary Fiber, g	3		
Protein, g	19		

Scallop Salad with Lime Vinaigrette

4 SERVINGS (1 1/2 CUPS EACH)

The scallops are cooked in white wine and lime juice instead of sautéed in butter for a zippy taste that blends perfectly with the vinaigrette.

1 pound scallops

1/2 cup dry white wine or fat-free chicken broth

2 tablespoons lime or lemon juice

1 cup shredded carrots (1 1/2 medium)

1 cup shredded daikon radish

1 tablespoon chopped fresh cilantro or parsley

1 large tomato, diced (1 1/2 cups)

2 tablespoons diced red or green bell pepper

2 tablespoons olive or vegetable oil

1 teaspoon dark sesame oil

2 tablespoons lime juice

2 teaspoons finely chopped fresh chives

2 teaspoons sugar, packed brown sugar or honey

1 teaspoon salt

1 teaspoon balsamic vinegar

1/4 teaspoon pepper

4 cups shredded romaine

If scallops are large, cut into fourths. Heat wine and 2 tablespoons lime juice to boiling in 10-inch nonstick skillet. Stir in scallops. Cook 2 to 3 minutes, stirring frequently, until scallops are white; drain. Toss scallops, carrots, radish, cilantro, tomato and bell pepper.

Beat oils, 2 tablespoons lime juice, the chives, sugar, salt, vinegar and pepper with wire whisk. Pour over scallop mixture; toss to coat evenly. Divide romaine among 4 plates. Spoon scallop mixture onto romaine.

1 Serving:		% Daily Value:	
Calories	240	Vitamin A	60%
Calories from fat	90	Vitamin C	26%
Fat, g	10	Calcium	16%
Saturated, g	1	Iron	24%
Cholesterol, mg	35	**Diet Exchanges:**	
Sodium, mg	860	Lean meat	3
Carbohydrate, g	13	Vegetable	2
Dietary Fiber, g	2		
Protein, g	27		

5

Meatless Mainstays

- Some dishes traditionally made with several eggs can be successfully made with only 1 or 2 whole eggs plus several egg whites. Some delicious examples of this technique are Popovers (page 159) and Apple-Cheese Oven Pancake (page 114).

- Use fat-free cholesterol-free egg products, available frozen and refrigerated, or egg whites instead of whole eggs. See page 212 for an egg white substitution chart and page 12 for guidelines on reducing the use of whole eggs.

- When cooking with cheese, use less than usual and use a reduced-fat cheese. The fat-free cheeses work best in recipes that don't require cooking, as they do not melt well.

- Canned beans are more convenient to use than dried; be sure to rinse and drain to remove excess sodium. Also, don't forget dried lentils, as they have a short cooking time compared to most dried beans.

- Enjoy a meal that does not contain meat at least once or twice a week.

Eggplant Lasagne (page 118)

Brunch Eggs on English Muffins

4 SERVINGS (WITH ABOUT 1/2 CUP SCRAMBLED EGG AND ABOUT 2 TABLESPOONS SAUCE EACH)

⏳ 🌢 ♥

With the reduced-fat cheeses available today, a lower-fat cheesy sauce is only a saucepan away.

Herbed Cheese Sauce (right)

2 English muffins, split

4 thin slices fully cooked Canadian-style bacon (2 ounces)

2 cups fat-free cholesterol-free egg product

Freshly ground pepper

Prepare Herbed Cheese Sauce; keep warm. Toast English muffins. Cook bacon in 10-inch nonstick skillet over medium heat until brown on both sides.

Spray 10-inch nonstick skillet with nonstick cooking spray. Heat over medium heat just until drop of water skitters when sprinkled in skillet. Pour egg product into skillet. As mixture begins to set at bottom and side, gently lift cooked portions with spatula so that thin, uncooked portion can flow to bottom. Avoid constant stirring. Cook 3 to 5 minutes or until thickened throughout but still moist.

Place 1 slice bacon on each muffin half. Top with eggs. Spoon about 2 tablespoons sauce over eggs. Sprinkle with pepper.

HERBED CHEESE SAUCE

1 teaspoon margarine or spread

2 teaspoons all-purpose flour

1/2 cup skim milk

1/4 cup shredded reduced-fat Cheddar cheese (1 ounce)

2 teaspoons grated reduced-fat Parmesan cheese blend

1/2 teaspoon chopped fresh or 1/4 teaspoon dried basil leaves

Dash of ground red pepper (cayenne)

Melt margarine in 1-quart nonstick saucepan over low heat. Stir in flour; remove from heat. Gradually stir in milk. Heat to boiling, stirring constantly. Boil and stir 1 minute; remove from heat. Stir in cheeses, basil and red pepper.

1 Serving:		% Daily Value:	
Calories	175	Vitamin A	10%
Calories from fat	35	Vitamin C	2%
Fat, g	4	Calcium	18%
Saturated, g	2	Iron	16%
Cholesterol, mg	10	**Diet Exchanges:**	
Sodium, mg	560	Starch/Bread	1
Carbohydrate, g	18	Lean meat	2
Dietary Fiber, g	2		
Protein, g	19		

Brunch Eggs on English Muffins

Apple-Cheese Oven Pancake

4 SERVINGS

Be sure to work quickly when making the apple filling while the pancake bakes. The pancake will deflate before you can fill it if the filling is not ready.

1 cup all-purpose flour

1 cup skim milk

1/4 teaspoon salt

2 eggs

4 egg whites

1 tablespoon margarine*

2 medium unpeeled tart cooking apples, thinly sliced (2 cups)

2 tablespoons chopped fresh or 2 teaspoons freeze-dried chives

2 tablespoons sugar

1/4 cup shredded reduced-fat Cheddar cheese (1 ounce)

Heat oven to 450°. Spray rectangular baking dish, 13×9×2 inches, with nonstick cooking spray. Beat flour, milk, salt, eggs and egg whites until smooth; pour into dish. Bake 15 to 20 minutes or until puffy and golden brown.

Meanwhile, melt margarine in 10-inch nonstick skillet over medium-high heat. Cook apples and chives in margarine, stirring frequently, until apples are tender. Stir in sugar. Spoon apple mixture onto pancake. Sprinkle with cheese. Bake about 1 minute or until cheese is melted.

*Do not use spreads or tub products.

1 Serving:		% Daily Value:	
Calories	290	Vitamin A	12%
Calories from fat	65	Vitamin C	4%
Fat, g	7	Calcium	14%
Saturated, g	2	Iron	10%
Cholesterol, mg	110	**Diet Exchanges:**	
Sodium, mg	320	Starch/Bread	2
Carbohydrate, g	45	Lean meat	1
Dietary Fiber, g	2	Fruit	1
Protein, g	14		

Apple-Cheese Oven Pancake

Scrambled Egg Pockets

4 SERVINGS

There are several egg-substitute products on the market today, both frozen and refrigerated. Check the labels; not all are fat free.

1 small tomato, chopped (1/2 cup)

1 small onion, chopped (1/4 cup)

2 tablespoons chopped green bell pepper

2 cups fat-free cholesterol-free egg product

1 teaspoon chopped fresh or 1/2 teaspoon dried tarragon leaves

1/4 teaspoon salt

2 pita breads (6 inches in diameter), cut in half and opened to form pockets

1/2 cup alfalfa sprouts

Spray 10-inch nonstick skillet with nonstick cooking spray. Cook tomato, onion and bell pepper in skillet over medium heat about 3 minutes, stirring frequently, until onion is tender. Mix egg product, tarragon and salt; pour into skillet.

As mixture begins to set at bottom and side, gently lift cooked portions with spatula so that thin, uncooked portion can flow to bottom. Avoid constant stirring. Cook 3 to 5 minutes or until eggs are thickened throughout but still moist. Spoon into pita breads. Top with alfalfa sprouts.

1 Serving:		% Daily Value:	
Calories	140	Vitamin A	8%
Calories from fat	10	Vitamin C	6%
Fat, g	1	Calcium	6%
Saturated, g	0	Iron	18%
Cholesterol, mg	0	**Diet Exchanges:**	
Sodium, mg	460	Starch/Bread	1
Carbohydrate, g	22	Lean meat	1
Dietary Fiber, g	2	Vegetable	1
Protein, g	13		

Potato-Basil Scramble

4 SERVINGS (ABOUT 1 CUP EACH)

2 cups cubed cooked potatoes (2 medium)

1 medium onion, finely chopped (1/2 cup)

1 small red bell pepper, chopped (1/2 cup)

2 cups fat-free cholesterol-free egg product

2 tablespoons chopped fresh or 2 teaspoons dried basil leaves

1/2 teaspoon salt

1/8 teaspoon ground red pepper (cayenne)

Spray 10-inch nonstick skillet with nonstick cooking spray. Cook potatoes, onion and bell pepper in skillet over medium heat about 5 minutes, stirring frequently, until hot. Mix remaining ingredients; pour into skillet.

As mixture begins to set at bottom and side, gently lift cooked portions with spatula so that thin, uncooked portion can flow to bottom. Avoid constant stirring. Cook 3 to 5 minutes or until eggs are thickened throughout but still moist.

1 Serving:		% Daily Value:	
Calories	115	Vitamin A	14%
Calories from fat	0	Vitamin C	26%
Fat, g	0	Calcium	4%
Saturated, g	0	Iron	14%
Cholesterol, mg	0	**Diet Exchanges:**	
Sodium, mg	440	Starch/Bread	1
Carbohydrate, g	20	Lean meat	1/2
Dietary Fiber, g	3	Vegetable	1
Protein, g	12		

Vegetable Manicotti

4 SERVINGS (2 MANICOTTI SHELLS EACH)

1 can (8 ounces) tomato sauce

8 uncooked manicotti shells

1 teaspoon olive or vegetable oil

1/2 cup shredded carrot (1 medium)

1/2 cup shredded zucchini

1/2 cup sliced mushrooms (1 1/2 ounces)

1/4 cup sliced green onions (3 medium)

1 clove garlic, finely chopped

1/4 cup grated reduced-fat Parmesan cheese blend

1/4 cup fat-free cholesterol-free egg product or 2 egg whites

2 tablespoons chopped fresh or 2 teaspoons dried basil leaves

1 container (15 ounces) fat-free ricotta cheese

1/2 cup shredded part-skim mozzarella cheese (2 ounces)

Heat oven to 350°. Spray rectangular baking dish, 11 × 7 × 1 1/2 inches, with nonstick cooking spray. Pour 1/3 cup of the tomato sauce into baking dish. Cook and drain manicotti shells as directed on package.

Heat oil in 10-inch nonstick skillet over medium-high heat. Cook carrot, zucchini, mushrooms, onions and garlic in oil, stirring frequently, until vegetables are crisp-tender. Stir in remaining ingredients except mozzarella cheese.

Fill manicotti shells with vegetable mixture; place in baking dish. Pour remaining tomato sauce over manicotti. Sprinkle with mozzarella cheese. Cover and bake 40 to 45 minutes or until hot and bubbly.

1 Serving:		% Daily Value:	
Calories	290	Vitamin A	42%
Calories from fat	54	Vitamin C	10%
Fat, g	6	Calcium	50%
Saturated, g	2	Iron	16%
Cholesterol, mg	27	Diet Exchanges:	
Sodium, mg	670	Starch/Bread	1
Carbohydrate, g	39	Medium-fat meat	1
Dietary Fiber, g	3	Vegetable	2
Protein, g	25	Skim milk	1

Eggplant Lasagne

8 SERVINGS

Eggplant plays the roll of the meat in this all-veggie rendition of the ever-popular lasagne.

1/2 cup dry sherry, fat-free chicken broth or vegetable broth

3 cups sliced mushrooms (8 ounces)

1 large onion, chopped (1 cup)

1 medium red bell pepper, chopped (1 cup)

2 cloves garlic, finely chopped

1/2 teaspoon salt

1/4 teaspoon pepper

1 1/2 cups fat-free ricotta cheese

1/4 cup fat-free cholesterol-free egg product or 2 egg whites

1 medium eggplant (1 1/2 pounds)

8 uncooked lasagne noodles

2 cups low-fat spaghetti sauce

1/2 cup shredded part-skim mozzarella cheese (2 ounces)

Heat oven to 350°. Spray rectangular pan, 13 × 9 × 2 inches, with nonstick cooking spray. Heat sherry to boiling in 10-inch nonstick skillet over medium-high heat. Cook mushrooms, onion, bell pepper and garlic in sherry 5 to 8 minutes, stirring frequently, until onion and bell pepper are tender. Stir in salt and pepper.

Mix ricotta cheese and egg product. Cut slice from top and bottom of eggplant. Cut eggplant lengthwise into 1/4-inch slices.

Spread half of the spaghetti sauce in bottom of pan. Top with half of the eggplant strips, half of the mushroom mixture and 4 uncooked noodles. Spread with ricotta cheese mixture. Repeat with remaining eggplant, mushroom mixture and noodles. Spread with remaining spaghetti sauce. Sprinkle with mozzarella cheese.

Cover and bake 45 minutes. Uncover and bake about 15 minutes longer or until bubbly and light brown. Let stand 5 minutes before cutting.

1 Serving:		% Daily Value:	
Calories	210	Vitamin A	16%
Calories from fat	35	Vitamin C	20%
Fat, g	4	Calcium	22%
Saturated, g	2	Iron	12%
Cholesterol, mg	15	**Diet Exchanges:**	
Sodium, mg	650	Starch/Bread	1
Carbohydrate, g	34	Vegetable	1
Dietary Fiber, g	3	Skim milk	1
Protein, g	12		

Easy Macaroni and Cheese

4 SERVINGS (ABOUT 3/4 CUP EACH)

⧗ ◓ ♥

1 package (7 ounces) pasta shells

1 tablespoon margarine or spread

2 tablespoons all-purpose flour

1/4 teaspoon salt

1/4 teaspoon ground mustard (dry)

1/8 teaspoon pepper

1 cup skim milk

1 cup shredded reduced-fat Cheddar cheese (4 ounces)

2 tablespoons sliced green onions

2 tablespoons chopped red bell pepper

Cook and drain pasta as directed on package. Meanwhile, melt margarine in 3-quart nonstick saucepan over low heat. Stir in flour, salt, mustard and pepper. Cook over low heat, stirring constantly, until margarine is absorbed; remove from heat. Gradually stir in milk. Heat to boiling, stirring constantly. Boil and stir 1 minute. Stir in cheese until melted.

Stir pasta, onions and bell pepper into sauce. Cook, stirring constantly, until hot.

1 Serving:		% Daily Value:	
Calories	330	Vitamin A	12%
Calories from fat	80	Vitamin C	6%
Fat, g	9	Calcium	30%
Saturated, g	4	Iron	12%
Cholesterol, mg	15	**Diet Exchanges:**	
Sodium, mg	350	Starch/Bread	2
Carbohydrate, g	46	Vegetable	1
Dietary Fiber, g	1	Skim milk	1
Protein, g	17	Fat	1

Enchilada Torta

4 SERVINGS

⧗ ◓ ♥

1 cup fat-free refried beans

1 can (4 ounces) chopped green chilies

1 small tomato, chopped (1/2 cup)

4 corn tortillas (6 inches in diameter)

1 1/4 cups green sauce

1 1/2 cups shredded reduced-fat Cheddar cheese (6 ounces)

Fat-free sour cream, if desired

Heat oven to 350°. Spray pie plate, 9 × 1 1/4 inches, with nonstick cooking spray. Mix beans, chilies and tomato. Place 1 tortilla in pie plate. Layer with one-fourth each of the bean mixture, green sauce and cheese. Repeat 3 times.

Cover loosely and bake 25 to 30 minutes or until cheese is melted and beans are heated through. Serve with sour cream.

1 Serving:		% Daily Value:	
Calories	260	Vitamin A	52%
Calories from fat	90	Vitamin C	42%
Fat, g	10	Calcium	40%
Saturated, g	5	Iron	12%
Cholesterol, mg	25	**Diet Exchanges:**	
Sodium, mg	1,340	Starch/Bread	2
Carbohydrate, g	32	Medium-fat meat	1
Dietary Fiber, g	7	Fat	1
Protein, g	18		

Whole Wheat Ratatouille Calzone

4 CALZONES

Pizza in a pocket! Although the whole family will love these, we think teens will especially find them fun to make and eat. (See teen party menu on page 21.)

Whole Wheat Dough (right)

2 teaspoons olive or vegetable oil

2 medium tomatoes, cut into eighths

1 small bell pepper, chopped (1/2 cup)

1 small onion, thinly sliced

2 cups 1/2-inch cubes eggplant

1 cup sliced zucchini

2 teaspoons chopped fresh or 1/2 teaspoon dried basil leaves

1 teaspoon chopped fresh or 1/4 teaspoon dried oregano leaves

1/2 teaspoon salt

1/4 teaspoon pepper

1 clove garlic, finely chopped

1 cup shredded part-skim mozzarella cheese (4 ounces)

2 tablespoons grated reduced-fat Parmesan cheese blend

1 egg white, beaten

Heat oven to 375°. Prepare Whole Wheat Dough.

Heat oil in 10-inch nonstick skillet over medium heat. Cook remaining ingredients except cheeses and egg white in oil, stirring frequently, until vegetables are tender and liquid has evaporated.

Spray cookie sheet with nonstick cooking spray. Divide dough into 4 equal pieces. Pat each piece into 8-inch circle on lightly floured surface, turning dough over occasionally to coat with flour. Top half of each circle with about 3/4 cup vegetable mixture to within 1 inch of edge. Sprinkle cheeses over vegetable mixture. Fold dough over vegetable mixture; fold edge up and pinch securely to seal. Place on cookie sheet. Brush with egg white. Bake about 25 minutes or until golden brown.

WHOLE WHEAT DOUGH

1 package regular or quick active dry yeast

3/4 cup warm water (105° to 115°)

1 tablespoon sugar

3/4 teaspoon salt

1 tablespoon olive or vegetable oil

1 3/4 to 2 1/4 cups whole wheat flour

Dissolve yeast in warm water in large bowl. Stir in sugar, salt, oil and 1 cup of the flour. Beat until smooth. Mix in enough remaining flour to make dough easy to handle. Turn dough onto lightly floured surface. Knead about 5 minutes or until smooth and elastic. Cover with bowl and let rest 5 minutes.

1 Calzone:		% Daily Value:	
Calories	370	Vitamin A	10%
Calories from fat	115	Vitamin C	22%
Fat, g	12	Calcium	28%
Saturated, g	5	Iron	18%
Cholesterol, mg	15	**Diet Exchanges:**	
Sodium, mg	890	Starch/Bread	3
Carbohydrate, g	52	High-fat meat	1
Dietary Fiber, g	8	Vegetable	1
Protein, g	19		

Whole Wheat Ratatouille Calzone, Zesty Fruit Salad (page 171), Almost Guacamole (page 30), Spicy Tortilla Chips (page 34)

Pita Pizzas

4 SERVINGS

⌛ 💧 ♥

4 whole wheat pita breads (4 inches in diameter)

1 can (15 to 16 ounces) great northern beans, drained and 1/4 cup liquid reserved

1 small onion, chopped (1/4 cup)

1 small clove garlic, finely chopped

2 tablespoons chopped fresh or 2 teaspoons dried basil leaves

1 large tomato, seeded and cut into 1/4-inch pieces

1 large green bell pepper, cut into 16 thin rings

1 cup shredded part-skim mozzarella cheese (4 ounces)

Heat oven to 425°. Cut pita breads around edge in half with knife. Place in ungreased jelly roll pan, 15 1/2 × 10 1/2 × 1 inch. Bake about 5 minutes or just until crisp.

Heat reserved bean liquid to boiling in 10-inch nonstick skillet over medium heat. Cook onion and garlic in liquid 5 minutes, stirring frequently. Stir in beans; heat through.

Place bean mixture and basil in blender or food processor. Cover and blend on medium speed until smooth. Spread about 2 tablespoons bean mixture on each pita bread half. Top each with tomato, bell pepper and cheese. Bake in jelly roll pan 5 to 7 minutes or until cheese is melted.

1 Serving:		% Daily Value:	
Calories	290	Vitamin A	8%
Calories from fat	55	Vitamin C	26%
Fat, g	6	Calcium	6%
Saturated, g	3	Iron	30%
Cholesterol, mg	15	**Diet Exchanges:**	
Sodium, mg	540	Starch/Bread	3
Carbohydrate, g	46	Lean meat	1
Dietary Fiber, g	8		
Protein, g	21		

Pesto Pizza on Focaccia

8 SERVINGS

1 Serving:		% Daily Value:	
Calories	235	Vitamin A	24%
Calories from fat	80	Vitamin C	28%
Fat, g	9	Calcium	20%
Saturated, g	3	Iron	16%
Cholesterol, mg	10	**Diet Exchanges:**	
Sodium, mg	730	Starch/Bread	1 1/2
Carbohydrate, g	31	Vegetable	2
Dietary Fiber, g	2	Fat	1
Protein, g	10		

Basil-Spinach Pesto (below)

1 round plain focaccia, flatbread or pizza crust (14 inches in diameter)

2 cups reduced-fat spaghetti sauce

1 medium green bell pepper, cut into rings

1 medium red bell pepper, cut into rings

1 cup shredded part-skim mozzarella cheese (4 ounces)

Heat oven to 500°. Prepare Basil-Spinach Pesto. Place focaccia on ungreased cookie sheet; spread with pesto. Top with spaghetti sauce and bell peppers. Sprinkle with cheese. Bake 10 to 15 minutes or until cheese is brown and bubbly.

BASIL-SPINACH PESTO

1/3 cup plain fat-free yogurt

1/3 cup soft bread crumbs

3 tablespoons grated reduced-fat Parmesan cheese blend

1 tablespoon olive or vegetable oil

2 cloves garlic, finely chopped

2 cups lightly packed fresh basil leaves

1 cup chopped spinach leaves

Place all ingredients in food processor in order listed. Cover and process about 2 minutes, stopping occasionally to scrape side of bowl, until mixture is a thick paste.

Rice-crusted Pizza

4 SERVINGS

Use this nifty pizza crust idea to carry any of your favorite pizza toppings.

1 1/2 cups cooked rice

1/4 cup fat-free cholesterol-free egg product or 2 egg whites

2/3 cup shredded part-skim mozzarella cheese

2 cups low-fat spaghetti sauce

1/2 medium green bell pepper, cut into rings

1/2 medium red bell pepper, cut into rings

1/4 cup chopped fresh or 1 teaspoon dried basil leaves

Heat oven to 450°. Spray square nonstick pan, 8 × 8 × 2 inches, with nonstick cooking spray. Mix rice, egg product and half of the cheese. Press evenly in bottom of pan. Bake about 15 minutes or until set.

Spread spaghetti sauce over crust. Top with bell peppers, basil and remaining cheese. Bake about 20 minutes or until cheese is brown and bubbly. Cool slightly before cutting.

1 Serving:		% Daily Value:	
Calories	205	Vitamin A	18%
Calories from fat	55	Vitamin C	26%
Fat, g	6	Calcium	20%
Saturated, g	2	Iron	12%
Cholesterol, mg	10	**Diet Exchanges:**	
Sodium, mg	930	Starch/Bread	2
Carbohydrate, g	30	Lean meat	1
Dietary Fiber, g	2		
Protein, g	10		

Bean Patties

4 SERVINGS

Yogurt sparked with horseradish makes an ideal accompaniment to this stand-in for the ubiquitous hamburger.

1 can (15 to 16 ounces) pinto beans, rinsed and well drained

1/2 cup shredded fat-free Cheddar cheese (2 ounces)

1/4 cup dry bread crumbs

2 tablespoons chopped green onions

1 teaspoon Worcestershire sauce

1/4 teaspoon pepper

1/8 teaspoon salt

2 tablespoons fat-free cholesterol-free egg product or 1 egg white

4 whole wheat hamburger buns, split

Horseradish Sauce (right)

4 slices tomato

4 lettuce leaves

Spray 10-inch nonstick skillet with nonstick cooking spray. Mash beans in medium bowl. Mix in cheese, bread crumbs, onions, Worcestershire sauce, pepper, salt and egg product. Shape mixture into 4 patties.

Cook patties in skillet over medium heat about 10 minutes, turning once, until light brown. Serve on buns with Horseradish Sauce, tomato and lettuce.

HORSERADISH SAUCE

1/2 cup plain fat-free yogurt

2 teaspoons prepared horseradish

Mix ingredients.

1 Serving:		% Daily Value:	
Calories	255	Vitamin A	6%
Calories from fat	10	Vitamin C	6%
Fat, g	1	Calcium	26%
Saturated, g	0	Iron	26%
Cholesterol, mg	0	**Diet Exchanges:**	
Sodium, mg	680	Starch/Bread	3
Carbohydrate, g	52	Vegetable	1
Dietary Fiber, g	10		
Protein, g	19		

Polenta Squares with Tomato Sauce

4 SERVINGS

1 cup yellow cornmeal

1 cup fat-free chicken broth, vegetable broth or water

3 cups boiling water

1/2 teaspoon salt

2 tablespoons grated reduced-fat Parmesan cheese blend

1 cup low-fat spaghetti sauce

2 tablespoons chopped fresh or 1 teaspoon dried basil leaves

1/2 cup shredded part-skim mozzarella cheese (2 ounces)

Mix cornmeal and broth in 2-quart saucepan. Stir in boiling water and salt. Cook over medium-high heat, stirring constantly, until mixture thickens and boils; reduce heat. Cover and simmer 10 minutes, stirring frequently; remove from heat. Stir in Parmesan cheese.

Spread polenta in ungreased nonstick square pan, 8 × 8 × 2 inches. Cover and refrigerate about 1 hour or until firm. Cut into 4 squares.

Set oven control to broil. Line broiler pan with aluminum foil. Spray both sides of polenta squares with nonstick cooking spray; place in broiler pan. Broil with tops of polenta about 4 inches from heat about 2 minutes each side or until light brown.

Spoon spaghetti sauce over squares in pan. Sprinkle with basil and mozzarella cheese. Broil about 2 minutes or until cheese is melted.

1 Square:		% Daily Value:	
Calories	185	Vitamin A	8%
Calories from fat	25	Vitamin C	2%
Fat, g	3	Calcium	16%
Saturated, g	1	Iron	10%
Cholesterol, mg	5	**Diet Exchanges:**	
Sodium, mg	800	Starch/Bread	2
Carbohydrate, g	33	Vegetable	1
Dietary Fiber, g	2		
Protein, g	8		

Polenta Squares with Tomato Sauce, Three-Grain Patties with Mushroom Sauce (page 129)

Polenta-Cheese Casserole

4 SERVINGS

1 cup yellow cornmeal

1 cup fat-free chicken broth, vegetable broth or water

3 cups boiling water

1/2 teaspoon salt

1 tablespoon margarine or spread

1 cup grated reduced-fat Parmesan cheese blend

1/3 cup shredded reduced-fat Swiss cheese

Heat oven to 350°. Spray 1 1/2-quart casserole with nonstick cooking spray. Mix cornmeal and broth in 2-quart saucepan. Stir in boiling water and salt. Cook over medium-high heat, stirring constantly, until mixture thickens and boils; reduce heat. Cover and simmer 10 minutes, stirring frequently; remove from heat. Stir until smooth.

Spread one-third of the cornmeal mixture in casserole. Dot with one-third of the margarine. Sprinkle with 1/3 cup of the Parmesan cheese. Repeat twice. Sprinkle with Swiss cheese. Bake uncovered about 20 minutes or until hot and bubbly.

1 Serving:		% Daily Value:	
Calories	210	Vitamin A	8%
Calories from fat	45	Vitamin C	0%
Fat, g	5	Calcium	38%
Saturated, g	2	Iron	8%
Cholesterol, mg	15	**Diet Exchanges:**	
Sodium, mg	680	Starch/Bread	1
Carbohydrate, g	28	Skim milk	1
Dietary Fiber, g	1	Fat	1
Protein, g	14		

Fruity Polenta

4 SERVINGS

To round out the meal, serve with Hummus (page 35) and Baked Pita Chips (page 34), along with a spinach salad.

1 cup yellow cornmeal

1 cup skim milk

3 cups boiling water

1/2 teaspoon salt

1/2 cup golden raisins

2 tablespoons shredded coconut

1 tablespoon honey

1/4 teaspoon curry powder

1 can (8 ounces) crushed pineapple in juice, well drained

1/4 cup chopped dry-roasted peanuts

Mix cornmeal and milk in 2-quart saucepan. Stir in boiling water and salt. Stir in remaining ingredients except peanuts. Cook over medium-high heat, stirring constantly, until mixture thickens and boils; reduce heat. Cover and simmer 10 minutes, stirring frequently; remove from heat. Stir until smooth. Sprinkle with peanuts.

1 Serving:		% Daily Value:	
Calories	295	Vitamin A	4%
Calories from fat	55	Vitamin C	4%
Fat, g	6	Calcium	10%
Saturated, g	2	Iron	12%
Cholesterol, mg	0	**Diet Exchanges:**	
Sodium, mg	350	Starch/Bread	2
Carbohydrate, g	56	Fruit	1 1/2
Dietary Fiber, g	4	Fat	1
Protein, g	8		

Three-Grain Patties with Mushroom Sauce

4 SERVINGS (2 PATTIES AND 1/4 CUP SAUCE EACH)

1/3 cup fat-free chicken broth or vegetable broth

1 medium onion, finely chopped (1/2 cup)

1/2 cup shredded carrot (1 medium)

1/2 cup shredded daikon radish or celery

1/4 cup fat-free cholesterol-free egg product or 2 egg whites

2 tablespoons finely chopped fresh parsley

1 1/2 tablespoons soy sauce

1/2 teaspoon finely chopped fresh or 1/4 teaspoon dried thyme leaves

1/4 teaspoon poultry seasoning

1/2 cup cooked white rice

1/2 cup cooked wild rice

1/4 cup cooked couscous, polenta or bulgur

1/2 slice whole wheat bread, crumbled

Mushroom Sauce (page 178)

1/2 teaspoon chopped fresh or 1/4 teaspoon dried thyme leaves

1 tablespoon Worcestershire sauce

Heat broth to boiling in 10-inch nonstick skillet over medium-high heat. Cook onion, carrot and radish in broth 5 to 8 minutes, stirring frequently, until tender; remove from heat. Place onion mixture in medium bowl. Stir in egg product, parsley, soy sauce, 1/2 teaspoon thyme, the poultry seasoning, rice, wild rice, couscous and bread crumbs. Shape mixture into 8 three-inch patties.

Prepare Mushroom Sauce—except substitute 1/2 teaspoon thyme for the tarragon and add Worcestershire sauce with the milk.

Spray clean skillet with nonstick cooking spray. Cook patties in skillet over medium heat, turning once, until crisp and brown. Serve with sauce.

1 Serving:		% Daily Value:	
Calories	160	Vitamin A	30%
Calories from fat	35	Vitamin C	6%
Fat, g	4	Calcium	10%
Saturated, g	1	Iron	10%
Cholesterol, mg	1	**Diet Exchanges:**	
Sodium, mg	760	Starch/Bread	1 1/2
Carbohydrate, g	26	Vegetable	1
Dietary Fiber, g	2		
Protein, g	7		

Meatless Chili Madness

There are as many ways to make chili as there are cooks. We've gathered three meatless recipes that offer a variety of tastes and ingredients. After you've tried them all, you'll be hard pressed to chose a favorite.

THREE-BEAN CHILI

4 SERVINGS

1 can (14 1/2 ounces) fat-free chicken broth or vegetable broth

1 large onion, chopped (1 cup)

2 cloves garlic, finely chopped

2 medium tomatoes, coarsely chopped (2 cups)

2 tablespoons chopped fresh cilantro

1 tablespoon chopped fresh or 1 teaspoon dried oregano leaves

2 teaspoons chili powder

1 teaspoon ground cumin

1 can (15 to 16 ounces) chili beans, undrained

1 can (8 ounces) kidney beans, undrained

1 can (8 ounces) garbanzo beans, undrained

Heat 1/4 cup of the broth to boiling in nonstick Dutch oven over medium heat. Cook onion and garlic in broth 5 minutes, stirring frequently.

Stir in remaining broth and remaining ingredients except beans. Heat to boiling; reduce heat. Cover and simmer 30 minutes, stirring occasionally.

Stir in all beans. Heat to boiling; reduce heat. Simmer uncovered about 20 minutes, stirring occasionally, until desired consistency.

1 Serving:		% Daily Value:	
Calories	225	Vitamin A	14%
Calories from fat	25	Vitamin C	22%
Fat, g	3	Calcium	10%
Saturated, g	0	Iron	30%
Cholesterol, mg	0	**Diet Exchanges:**	
Sodium, mg	1,050	Starch/Bread	3
Carbohydrate, g	45		
Dietary Fiber, g	12		
Protein, g	16		

WHITE BEAN CHILI

6 SERVINGS

Tomatillo Salsa (right)

1 can (14 1/2 ounces) fat-free chicken
    broth or vegetable broth

1 large onion, chopped (1 cup)

1 medium yellow bell pepper, chopped
    (1 cup)

2 jalapeño chilies, seeded and chopped

2 cloves garlic, finely chopped

1 1/2 cups water

1 teaspoon grated lime peel

2 tablespoons lime juice

1 teaspoon cumin seed

1/2 teaspoon dried oregano leaves

1/2 teaspoon ground coriander

1/4 teaspoon salt

1 can (15 to 16 ounces) great northern
    beans, rinsed and drained

1 can (15 to 16 ounces) butter beans,
    rinsed and drained

1 can (15 to 16 ounces) black-eyed
    peas, rinsed and drained

Prepare Tomatillo Salsa. Heat half of the
broth to boiling in Dutch oven. Cook onion,
bell pepper, chilies and garlic in broth, stirring frequently, until onion is tender. Stir in
remaining broth and remaining ingredients.
Heat to boiling; reduce heat. Simmer uncovered 20 minutes. Serve with salsa.

TOMATILLO SALSA

1/4 cup chopped green onions
    (3 medium)

1/4 cup chopped fresh cilantro

2 tablespoons pine nuts, toasted

1 tablespoon lime juice

1/4 teaspoon salt

8 ounces tomatillos or roma (plum)
    tomatoes, chopped

1 jalapeño chili, seeded and chopped

Mix all ingredients. Cover and refrigerate at
least 30 minutes to blend flavors.

1 Serving:		% Daily Value:	
Calories	250	Vitamin A	30%
Calories from fat	25	Vitamin C	66%
Fat, g	3	Calcium	10%
Saturated, g	1	Iron	36%
Cholesterol, mg	0	**Diet Exchanges:**	
Sodium, mg	870	Starch/Bread	3
Carbohydrate, g	52	Vegetable	1
Dietary Fiber, g	16		
Protein, g	19		

(Continued on next page)

BAKED CHILI IN POLENTA CRUST

6 SERVINGS

Polenta Crust (right)

1 teaspoon vegetable oil

1 medium onion, chopped (1/2 cup)

1 clove garlic, finely chopped

1 can (15 ounces) tomato sauce

1 can (6 ounces) tomato paste

1 can (15 to 16 ounces) pinto beans, rinsed and drained

1 can (15 ounces) black beans, rinsed and drained

1 tablespoon chili powder

1 teaspoon ground cumin

1/4 teaspoon ground cinnamon

1/4 teaspoon pepper

1/2 cup shredded sharp reduced-fat Cheddar cheese (2 ounces)

Prepare Polenta Crust. Heat oven to 350°. Grease 2-quart casserole. Heat oil in 2-quart nonstick saucepan over medium heat. Cook onion and garlic in oil about 5 minutes, stirring frequently, until onion is crisp-tender. Stir in remaining ingredients except cheese. Heat to boiling, stirring frequently.

Spread or press crust mixture on bottom and up side of casserole to form crust. Spoon chili mixture into crust. Bake uncovered 30 to 35 minutes or until hot. Sprinkle with cheese. Bake uncovered 2 to 3 minutes or until cheese is melted.

POLENTA CRUST

1 cup yellow cornmeal

3/4 cup skim milk

3 1/4 cups boiling water

1 teaspoon salt

3 tablespoons canned chopped green chilies

Mix cornmeal and milk in 2-quart saucepan. Stir in boiling water and salt. Cook over medium-high heat, stirring constantly, until mixture thickens and boils; reduce heat. Cover and simmer 10 minutes, stirring frequently; remove from heat. Stir in chilies. Cool about 30 minutes or until set.

1 Serving:		% Daily Value:	
Calories	325	Vitamin A	22%
Calories from fat	35	Vitamin C	22%
Fat, g	4	Calcium	22%
Saturated, g	2	Iron	34%
Cholesterol, mg	5	**Diet Exchanges:**	
Sodium, mg	1,440	Starch/Bread	4
Carbohydrate, g	66	Vegetable	1
Dietary Fiber, g	13		
Protein, g	19		

Red Pepper and Broccoli Risotto

4 SERVINGS (ABOUT 1 1/2 CUPS EACH)

4 1/2 cups fat-free chicken broth or vegetable broth

1 large onion, chopped (1 cup)

4 cloves garlic, finely chopped

2 medium red bell peppers, chopped (2 cups)

2 cups sliced mushrooms (6 ounces)

1 1/2 cups uncooked arborio or other short-grain white rice

2 cups broccoli flowerets

1 teaspoon salt

3 tablespoons grated reduced-fat Parmesan cheese blend

1/3 cup chopped fresh parsley

Spray 2-quart nonstick saucepan with nonstick cooking spray. Heat 1/4 cup of the broth to boiling in saucepan. Cook onion, garlic, bell peppers and mushrooms in broth 3 to 5 minutes, stirring frequently, until onions are crisp-tender. Stir in rice. Cook 1 minute, stirring constantly.

Stir in 1/2 cup of the broth. Cook, stirring constantly, until liquid is completely absorbed. Stir in an additional 1/2 cup broth. Continue cooking about 20 minutes, adding broth 1/2 cup at a time after previous additions have been absorbed and stirring constantly, until rice is creamy and just tender; remove from heat. Stir in remaining ingredients. Cook 1 minute.

1 Serving:		% Daily Value:	
Calories	340	Vitamin A	28%
Calories from fat	10	Vitamin C	96%
Fat, g	1	Calcium	12%
Saturated, g	0	Iron	24%
Cholesterol, mg	2	**Diet Exchanges:**	
Sodium, mg	1,490	Starch/Bread	4
Carbohydrate, g	72	Vegetable	2
Dietary Fiber, g	4		
Protein, g	15		

Spicy Rice with Black-eyed Peas

4 SERVINGS (ABOUT 1 1/4 CUPS EACH)

l package (10 ounces) frozen black-eyed peas*

3/4 cup uncooked instant rice

1/4 cup chopped red bell pepper

1 tablespoon chopped fresh or 1 teaspoon dried oregano leaves

1/4 teaspoon salt

1/8 teaspoon ground red pepper (cayenne)

1 medium onion, chopped (1/2 cup)

1 clove garlic, finely chopped

1 can (16 ounces) whole tomatoes, undrained

Cook peas as directed on package, using 10-inch nonstick skillet; drain. Stir in remaining ingredients, breaking up tomatoes. Heat to boiling; reduce heat. Cover and simmer about 10 minutes or until liquid is almost absorbed.

*1 can (15 to 16 ounces) black-eyed peas, drained, can be substituted for the frozen black-eyed peas. Do not cook before mixing with remaining ingredients.

1 Serving:		% Daily Value:	
Calories	165	Vitamin A	16%
Calories from fat	10	Vitamin C	26%
Fat, g	1	Calcium	12%
Saturated, g	0	Iron	12%
Cholesterol, mg	0	**Diet Exchanges:**	
Sodium, mg	320	Starch/Bread	2
Carbohydrate, g	38		
Dietary Fiber, g	4		
Protein, g	5		

Curried Lentils and Barley

4 SERVINGS (ABOUT 1 CUP EACH)

2 teaspoons vegetable oil

1 medium onion, chopped (1/2 cup)

1/3 cup coarsely chopped red or green bell pepper

3 1/2 cups water

1/2 cup uncooked barley

1 1/2 teaspoons curry powder

3/4 teaspoon salt

2 medium carrots, thinly sliced (1 cup)

3/4 cup dried lentils, sorted and rinsed

1/2 cup plain fat-free yogurt

1/4 cup chutney

Heat oil in 3-quart nonstick saucepan over medium-high heat. Cook onion and bell pepper in oil, stirring frequently, until crisp-tender. Stir in water, barley, curry powder and salt. Heat to boiling; reduce heat. Cover and simmer 15 minutes.

Stir in carrots and lentils. Heat to boiling; reduce heat. Cover and simmer 40 to 45 minutes, stirring occasionally, until lentils are tender and liquid is absorbed. Mix yogurt and chutney. Serve with lentil mixture.

1 Serving:		% Daily Value:	
Calories	260	Vitamin A	52%
Calories from fat	25	Vitamin C	18%
Fat, g	3	Calcium	10%
Saturated, g	1	Iron	26%
Cholesterol, mg	0	**Diet Exchanges:**	
Sodium, mg	450	Starch/Bread	2
Carbohydrate, g	54	Vegetable	2
Dietary Fiber, g	10		
Protein, g	14		

Fennel and Black Beans with Couscous

4 SERVINGS

Fennel is a fabulous herb that produces a root you can use like celery—either fresh or cooked. It has an anise flavor that adds a Mediterranean touch to the already exotic combination of black beans and couscous.

1 teaspoon olive or vegetable oil

1 medium red onion, thinly sliced

1 large red bell pepper, cut crosswise in half and thinly sliced

1 small bulb fennel, cut into fourths and thinly sliced

2 tablespoons chopped fresh or 2 teaspoons dried oregano leaves

1/4 teaspoon crushed red pepper

2 cans (15 ounces each) black beans, rinsed and drained

2 cups hot cooked couscous

Heat oil in 10-inch nonstick skillet over medium-high heat. Cook onion, bell pepper and fennel in oil 2 to 3 minutes, stirring frequently, until crisp-tender. Stir in oregano, red pepper and beans; reduce heat. Simmer uncovered 5 minutes. Serve with couscous.

1 Serving:		% Daily Value:	
Calories	365	Vitamin A	16%
Calories from fat	25	Vitamin C	48%
Fat, g	3	Calcium	18%
Saturated, g	1	Iron	30%
Cholesterol, mg	0	**Diet Exchanges:**	
Sodium, mg	690	Starch/Bread	5
Carbohydrate, g	80	Vegetable	1
Dietary Fiber, g	17		
Protein, g	21		

Mediterranean Couscous

4 SERVINGS

2 teaspoons margarine or spread

1/3 cup chopped green onions (4 medium)

1 clove garlic, finely chopped

1 1/2 cups water

1/2 teaspoon low-sodium chicken bouillon granules

1 cup uncooked couscous

1/4 cup chopped fresh parsley

1 tablespoon chopped fresh or 1/2 teaspoon dried basil leaves

1/4 teaspoon pepper

1 medium yellow summer squash, chopped (1 cup)

1 medium tomato, chopped (3/4 cup)

Melt margarine in 2-quart nonstick saucepan over medium-high heat. Cook onions and garlic in margarine, stirring frequently, until onions are tender. Stir in water and bouillon granules. Heat to boiling; remove from heat.

Stir in remaining ingredients. Cover and let stand about 5 minutes or until liquid is absorbed. Fluff lightly with fork.

1 Serving:		% Daily Value:	
Calories	205	Vitamin A	8%
Calories from fat	25	Vitamin C	14%
Fat, g	3	Calcium	4%
Saturated, g	1	Iron	6%
Cholesterol, mg	0	**Diet Exchanges:**	
Sodium, mg	35	Starch/Bread	2
Carbohydrate, g	40	Vegetable	2
Dietary Fiber, g	3		
Protein, g	7		

Mediterranean Couscous, Szechuan Vegetables with Rice (page 138)

Szechuan Vegetables with Rice

4 SERVINGS (1 1/2 CUPS EACH)

2 tablespoons soy sauce

1 teaspoon sugar

1 teaspoon cornstarch

1 teaspoon rice vinegar

1 jalapeño chili, finely chopped

1/2 to 3/4 cup fat-free chicken broth or vegetable broth

2 tablespoons dry sherry, sake or water

1 very large onion, thinly sliced (2 cups)

4 cloves garlic, finely chopped

1 tablespoon grated gingerroot

1 small eggplant, diced (3 cups)

1 medium red or yellow bell pepper, cut into julienne strips

1 cup thinly sliced napa (Chinese) cabbage, green cabbage or daikon radish

1/2 cup whole kernel corn

1/2 cup sliced Chinese pea pods

2 cups hot cooked rice

Mix soy sauce, sugar, cornstarch, vinegar and chili; set aside. Spray 10-inch nonstick skillet or wok with nonstick cooking spray. Heat over medium-high heat. Cook broth, sherry, onion, garlic and gingerroot in skillet 5 to 8 minutes, stirring frequently, until onion is tender.

Stir in eggplant, bell pepper, cabbage and corn. Cook 3 to 5 minutes, stirring frequently, until eggplant is tender. Stir in pea pods and cornstarch mixture. Cook, stirring constantly, until sauce thickens slightly. Serve over rice.

1 Serving:		% Daily Value:	
Calories	210	Vitamin A	28%
Calories from fat	10	Vitamin C	64%
Fat, g	1	Calcium	6%
Saturated, g	0	Iron	14%
Cholesterol, mg	0	**Diet Exchanges:**	
Sodium, mg	630	Starch/Bread	2 1/2
Carbohydrate, g	48	Vegetable	1
Dietary Fiber, g	5		
Protein, g	7		

Steamed Vegetables in Peanut Sauce with Rice

4 SERVINGS (1 1/2 CUPS EACH)

1 Japanese eggplant, cut into 2 × 1/2-inch strips (3 cups)

1 red bell pepper, cut into julienne strips (1 1/2 cups)

1 large carrot, cut into julienne strips (1 cup)

1 cup sliced bok choy or celery

1 medium onion, thinly sliced

2 tablespoons soy sauce

1 tablespoon smooth peanut butter

1 tablespoon hoisin sauce

1 teaspoon grated gingerroot

1 clove garlic, finely chopped

8 ounces Chinese pea pods, strings removed

2 cups hot cooked basmati or brown rice

Place steamer basket in 1/2 inch water in saucepan or skillet (water should not touch bottom of basket). Place eggplant, bell pepper, carrot, bok choy and onion in steamer basket. Cover tightly and heat to boiling; reduce heat. Steam 5 to 8 minutes or until vegetables are tender.

Meanwhile, mix soy sauce, peanut butter, hoisin sauce, gingerroot and garlic in large bowl. Add pea pods to vegetables in steamer basket; cover and steam 1 minute. Add vegetables to peanut butter mixture; toss. Serve over rice.

1 Serving:		% Daily Value:	
Calories	215	Vitamin A	60%
Calories from fat	25	Vitamin C	70%
Fat, g	3	Calcium	8%
Saturated, g	1	Iron	20%
Cholesterol, mg	0	**Diet Exchanges:**	
Sodium, mg	560	Starch/Bread	2 1/2
Carbohydrate, g	45	Vegetable	1
Dietary Fiber, g	6		
Protein, g	8		

Hearty Bean and Pasta Stew

4 SERVINGS (ABOUT 1 CUP EACH)

1 large tomato, coarsely chopped (1 cup)

1 small onion, chopped (1/4 cup)

1 clove garlic, finely chopped

3/4 cup uncooked pasta shells

1/4 cup chopped green bell pepper

1 tablespoon chopped fresh or 1 teaspoon dried basil leaves

1 teaspoon Worcestershire sauce

1 can (15 to 16 ounces) kidney beans, drained

1 can (8 ounces) garbanzo beans, drained

1 can (14 1/2 ounces) fat-free chicken broth or vegetable broth

Mix all ingredients in 2-quart saucepan. Heat to boiling, stirring frequently; reduce heat. Cover and simmer about 15 minutes, stirring occasionally, until pasta is tender.

1 Serving:		% Daily Value:	
Calories	245	Vitamin A	4%
Calories from fat	10	Vitamin C	14%
Fat, g	1	Calcium	6%
Saturated, g	0	Iron	28%
Cholesterol, mg	0	**Diet Exchanges:**	
Sodium, mg	810	Starch/Bread	3
Carbohydrate, g	52	Vegetable	1
Dietary Fiber, g	9		
Protein, g	16		

Vegetable Curried Rice

4 SERVINGS (ABOUT 1 1/2 CUPS EACH)

⧗ ◗ ♥

Don't let the long list of ingredients scare you off. This is an easy, one-pot dish that's ready in no time because it uses instant rice.

1 can (14 1/2 ounces) fat-free chicken broth or vegetable broth

1 medium onion, chopped (1/2 cup)

3 cloves garlic, finely chopped

1 cup shredded carrots (1 1/2 medium)

1 cup sliced mushrooms (3 ounces)

2 teaspoons curry powder

1/2 teaspoon ground cinnamon

1/4 teaspoon ground cumin

1/4 teaspoon ground coriander

1/4 cup chopped dried apricots

1/4 cup currants or raisins

1/2 teaspoon salt

2 cups uncooked instant rice

1/2 cup plain fat-free yogurt

1 medium tomato, diced (1 cup)

Plain fat-free yogurt, if desired

Mango chutney, if desired

Heat 1/4 cup of the broth to boiling in 3-quart nonstick saucepan over medium-high heat. Cook onion, garlic, carrots, mushrooms, curry powder, cinnamon, cumin and coriander in broth 5 to 8 minutes, stirring frequently, until onion is tender and liquid has evaporated.

Add enough water to remaining broth to make 2 cups. Stir broth mixture, apricots, currants and salt into vegetable mixture. Heat to boiling. Stir in rice; remove from heat. Cover and let stand about 5 minutes or until liquid is absorbed. Stir in 1/2 cup yogurt and the tomato. Serve with additional yogurt and chutney.

1 Serving:		% Daily Value:	
Calories	305	Vitamin A	50%
Calories from fat	0	Vitamin C	10%
Fat, g	0	Calcium	12%
Saturated, g	0	Iron	22%
Cholesterol, mg	0	**Diet Exchanges:**	
Sodium, mg	640	Starch/Bread	4
Carbohydrate, g	70		
Dietary Fiber, g	4		
Protein, g	10		

Gazpacho with Basil Cream

4 SERVINGS (ABOUT 1 3/4 CUP EACH)

The traditional garnish of hard-cooked eggs is replaced here with the fresh-tasting blend of basil and fat-free sour cream. Although gazpacho is usually served cold, this is also delicious hot.

2 large tomatoes, seeded and chopped (2 cups)

1 large red bell pepper, chopped (1 1/2 cups)

1 medium cucumber, peeled and chopped (1 cup)

1 medium stalk celery, diagonally sliced (1/2 cup)

1/4 cup sliced green onions (3 medium)

2 cups tomato juice

2 tablespoons red wine vinegar

1 to 2 teaspoons red pepper sauce

1/4 teaspoon freshly ground pepper

1/4 teaspoon Worcestershire sauce

1 clove garlic, finely chopped

1 can (15 ounces) black beans, rinsed and drained

Basil Cream (right)

1/4 cup herb-flavored croutons, if desired

Mix all ingredients except Basil Cream and croutons. Cover and refrigerate 4 to 6 hours to blend flavors, stirring occasionally. Top each serving with Basil Cream and croutons.

BASIL CREAM

1/2 cup fat-free sour cream

2 tablespoons chopped fresh or 1 teaspoon dried basil leaves

Mix ingredients.

1 Serving:		% Daily Value:	
Calories	215	Vitamin A	42%
Calories from fat	25	Vitamin C	98%
Fat, g	3	Calcium	14%
Saturated, g	1	Iron	22%
Cholesterol, mg	10	**Diet Exchanges:**	
Sodium, mg	730	Starch/Bread	2
Carbohydrate, g	44	Vegetable	2
Dietary Fiber, g	10		
Protein, g	13		

Lentil Stew

6 SERVINGS (ABOUT 1 1/3 CUPS EACH)

Perfectly seasoned with a touch of cumin and mace, this is a hearty meal for an incredibly low two grams of fat per serving.

2 teaspoons vegetable oil

2 medium onions, chopped (1 cup)

1 clove garlic, finely chopped

1 cup dried lentils, sorted and rinsed

3 cups water

1/4 cup chopped fresh parsley

1/2 teaspoon ground cumin

1/2 teaspoon salt

1/4 teaspoon pepper

1/4 teaspoon ground mace

2 medium potatoes, coarsely chopped (2 cups)

8 ounces small whole mushrooms, cut in half

1 can (28 ounces) whole tomatoes, undrained

Heat oil in Dutch oven over medium-high heat. Cook onions and garlic in oil, stirring frequently, until onions are crisp-tender. Stir in remaining ingredients, breaking up tomatoes. Heat to boiling; reduce heat. Cover and simmer about 40 minutes, stirring occasionally, until potatoes are tender.

1 Serving:		% Daily Value:	
Calories	180	Vitamin A	8%
Calories from fat	20	Vitamin C	26%
Fat, g	2	Calcium	6%
Saturated, g	0	Iron	26%
Cholesterol, mg	0	**Diet Exchanges:**	
Sodium, mg	400	Starch/Bread	2
Carbohydrate, g	38	Vegetable	1
Dietary Fiber, g	8		
Protein, g	11		

Black Bean Salad

4 SERVINGS (ABOUT 1 CUP EACH)

1 cup frozen whole kernel corn, thawed

1 cup diced jicama

1 medium tomato, seeded and chopped (3/4 cup)

2 green onions, sliced

2 cans (15 ounces each) black beans, rinsed and drained

Chili Dressing (below)

Toss all ingredients in large glass or plastic bowl. Cover and refrigerate at least 2 hours, stirring occasionally.

CHILI DRESSING

1/4 cup red wine vinegar

2 tablespoons vegetable oil

1/2 teaspoon chili powder

1/4 teaspoon ground cumin

1 small clove garlic, crushed

Mix all ingredients.

1 Serving:		% Daily Value:	
Calories	345	Vitamin A	4%
Calories from fat	70	Vitamin C	28%
Fat, g	8	Calcium	14%
Saturated, g	2	Iron	30%
Cholesterol, mg	0	**Diet Exchanges:**	
Sodium, mg	470	Starch/Bread	4
Carbohydrate, g	65	Vegetable	1
Dietary Fiber, g	16		
Protein, g	19		

Black Bean Salad, Wheat Berry Salad (page 144)

Wheat Berry Salad

4 SERVINGS (ABOUT 1 1/3 CUPS EACH)

Wheat berries are simply whole grains of wheat and can be found in the health food section of your local supermarket. Brown rice is also tasty in this salad; increase water to 2 3/4 cups.

1 cup uncooked wheat berries

2 1/2 cups water

1 1/2 cups broccoli flowerets

1/2 cup chopped green onions (5 medium)

1 medium carrot, diced (1/2 cup)

1 can (15 to 16 ounces) garbanzo beans, rinsed and drained

Vinaigrette Dressing (right)

Heat wheat berries and water to boiling in 2-quart saucepan, stirring once or twice; reduce heat. Cover and simmer 50 to 60 minutes or until wheat berries are tender but still firm; drain if necessary.

Toss wheat berries and remaining ingredients. Cover and refrigerate at least 1 hour.

VINAIGRETTE DRESSING

1/4 cup balsamic or cider vinegar

2 tablespoons olive or vegetable oil

1 tablespoon chopped fresh or 1 teaspoon dried basil leaves

1/4 teaspoon paprika

1/8 teaspoon salt

1 clove garlic, finely chopped

Shake all ingredients in tightly covered container.

1 Serving:		% Daily Value:	
Calories	300	Vitamin A	26%
Calories from fat	90	Vitamin C	60%
Fat, g	10	Calcium	8%
Saturated, g	1	Iron	24%
Cholesterol, mg	0	**Diet Exchanges:**	
Sodium, mg	320	Starch/Bread	3
Carbohydrate, g	48	Vegetable	1
Dietary Fiber, g	9	Fat	1
Protein, g	13		

Curried Couscous Salad

4 SERVINGS

1 cup fat-free chicken broth or vegetable broth

2/3 cup uncooked couscous

1 teaspoon curry powder

1/3 cup plain fat-free yogurt

2 tablespoons frozen (thawed) orange juice concentrate

1 teaspoon honey or sugar

1/2 teaspoon ground cumin

2 cups shredded salad greens (romaine, endive)

1 cup shredded carrots (1 1/2 medium)

1/2 cup raisins

1 medium tart apple, diced (1 cup)

1/4 cup chopped fresh cilantro

Heat broth to boiling in 2-quart saucepan over medium-high heat. Stir in couscous and curry powder; remove from heat. Cover and let stand 5 minutes.

Mix yogurt, juice concentrate, honey and cumin in large bowl. Add salad greens, carrots, raisins and apple; toss. Divide among 4 salad plates. Spoon one-fourth of the couscous onto center of each plate. Sprinkle with cilantro.

1 Serving:		% Daily Value:	
Calories	240	Vitamin A	44%
Calories from fat	10	Vitamin C	30%
Fat, g	1	Calcium	8%
Saturated, g	0	Iron	8%
Cholesterol, mg	0	**Diet Exchanges:**	
Sodium, mg	230	Starch/Bread	3
Carbohydrate, g	53	Vegetable	1
Dietary Fiber, g	3		
Protein, g	8		

6

Breads, Sides and Sauces

- Develop the habit of eating bread without butter or margarine. Many breads, eaten by themselves, are not high in fat.

- Experiment with adding applesauce in place of all or some of the fat in your favorite bread recipes. See page 25 for guidelines.

- Double the amount of vegetables, fruits and grain-based foods eaten with meals and reduce the amount of meat.

- Fresh herbs and spices are superb on vegetables in the place of rich sauces. Or, use the low-fat White Sauce on page 178 as the basis of a creamy sauce.

- Use highly flavored ingredients when making salad dressings and reduce or eliminate the oil. Balsamic vinegar, herb and fruit vinegars, peppercorns, chilies and fresh herbs all make for memorable vinaigrettes.

Three-Pepper Stir-fry (page 170),
Popovers (page 159)

Sour Cream Coffee Cake

16 SERVINGS

We've used applesauce and fat-free sour cream to tame the fat monster in everyone's favorite brunch bread—coffee cake.

Brown Sugar Filling (right)

1 1/2 cups sugar

1/2 cup margarine or spread

1/4 cup unsweetened applesauce

2 teaspoons vanilla

3 large eggs

3 cups all-purpose or whole wheat flour

1 1/2 teaspoons baking powder

1 1/2 teaspoons baking soda

3/4 teaspoon salt

1 1/2 cups fat-free sour cream

Vanilla Glaze (right)

Heat oven to 350°. Grease bottom and side of angel food cake pan (tube pan), 10 × 4 inches, with shortening. Prepare Brown Sugar Filling; set aside.

Beat sugar, margarine, applesauce, vanilla and eggs in large bowl with electric mixer on medium speed 2 minutes, scraping bowl occasionally. Mix flour, baking powder, baking soda and salt. Beat flour mixture and sour cream alternately into sugar mixture on low speed until blended (batter may look curdled). Spread one-third of the batter (about 2 cups) in pan, then sprinkle with one-third of the filling; repeat twice.

Bake about 1 hour or until toothpick inserted near center comes out clean. Cool slightly; remove from pan to wire rack. Cool 10 minutes. Drizzle with Vanilla Glaze. Serve warm or cool.

BROWN SUGAR FILLING

1/2 cup packed brown sugar

1/2 cup finely chopped nuts

1 1/2 teaspoons ground cinnamon

Mix all ingredients.

VANILLA GLAZE

1/2 cup powdered sugar

1/4 teaspoon vanilla

2 to 3 teaspoons milk

Mix all ingredients until smooth and drizzling consistency.

1 Serving:		% Daily Value:	
Calories	300	Vitamin A	12%
Calories from fat	80	Vitamin C	0%
Fat, g	9	Calcium	8%
Saturated, g	2	Iron	9%
Cholesterol, mg	45	**Diet Exchanges:**	
Sodium, mg	370	Starch/Bread	3
Carbohydrate, g	51	Fruit	1/2
Dietary Fiber, g	1	Fat	1
Protein, g	5		

Sour Cream Coffee Cake, Zucchini-Apricot Bread (page 150)

Pumpkin-Fruit Bread

1 LOAF (24 SLICES)

1 cup canned pumpkin

2/3 cup packed brown sugar

3 tablespoons vegetable oil

1 teaspoon vanilla

1/2 cup fat-free cholesterol-free egg product or 3 egg whites

1 1/2 cups all-purpose flour

1/2 cup diced dried fruit and raisin mixture

2 teaspoons baking powder

3/4 teaspoon ground cinnamon

1/2 teaspoon salt

1/4 teaspoon ground cloves

Heat oven to 350°. Spray loaf pan, 9 × 5 × 3 or 8 1/2 × 4 1/2 × 2 1/2 inches, with nonstick cooking spray. Mix pumpkin, brown sugar, oil, vanilla and egg product in large bowl. Stir in remaining ingredients just until moistened. Pour into pan.

Bake 50 to 60 minutes or until toothpick inserted in center comes out clean. Cool 5 minutes. Loosen sides of loaf from pan; remove from pan to wire rack. Cool completely before slicing. Store tightly wrapped in refrigerator up to 1 week.

1 Slice:		% Daily Value:	
Calories	80	Vitamin A	22%
Calories from fat	20	Vitamin C	0%
Fat, g	2	Calcium	4%
Saturated, g	0	Iron	4%
Cholesterol, mg	0	**Diet Exchanges:**	
Sodium, mg	95	Starch/Bread	1
Carbohydrate, g	15		
Dietary Fiber, g	0		
Protein, g	1		

Zucchini-Apricot Bread

1 LOAF (24 SLICES)

1 1/2 cups shredded zucchini (1 medium)

3/4 cup sugar

1/4 cup vegetable oil

1/2 cup fat-free cholesterol-free egg product or 3 egg whites

1 1/2 cups all-purpose flour

1 teaspoon ground cinnamon

2 teaspoons vanilla

3/4 teaspoon baking soda

1/2 teaspoon salt

1/4 teaspoon baking powder

1/4 teaspoon ground cloves

1/2 cup finely chopped dried apricots

Heat oven to 350°. Spray loaf pan, 8 1/2 × 4 1/2 × 2 1/2 or 9 × 5 × 3 inches, with nonstick cooking spray. Mix zucchini, sugar, oil and egg product in large bowl. Stir in remaining ingredients except apricots. Stir in apricots. Pour into pan.

Bake 60 to 70 minutes or until toothpick inserted in center comes out clean. Cool 10 minutes. Loosen sides of loaf from pan; remove from pan to wire rack. Cool completely before slicing. Store tightly wrapped in refrigerator up to 1 week.

1 Slice:		% Daily Value:	
Calories	80	Vitamin A	2%
Calories from fat	20	Vitamin C	0%
Fat, g	2	Calcium	0%
Saturated, g	0	Iron	4%
Cholesterol, mg	0	**Diet Exchanges:**	
Sodium, mg	95	Starch/Bread	1
Carbohydrate, g	15		
Dietary Fiber, g	0		
Protein, g	1		

Cranberry Bread

2 LOAVES (24 SLICES EACH)

Unsweetened applesauce replaces the fat for a very cranberry seasonal favorite.

3 cups fresh or frozen (thawed and drained) cranberries

1 2/3 cups sugar

2/3 cup unsweetened applesauce

1/2 cup milk

2 teaspoons grated lemon or orange peel

2 teaspoons vanilla

1 cup fat-free cholesterol-free egg product or 2 eggs plus 4 egg whites

3 cups all-purpose flour

2 teaspoons baking soda

1 teaspoon salt

1/2 teaspoon baking powder

Move oven rack to low position so that tops of pans will be in center of oven. Heat oven to 350°. Grease bottoms only of 2 loaf pans, 8 1/2 × 4 1/2 × 2 1/2 or 9 × 5 × 3 inches, with shortening. Mix cranberries, sugar, applesauce, milk, lemon peel, vanilla and egg product in large bowl. Stir in remaining ingredients. Pour into pans.

Bake 60 to 70 minutes or until toothpick inserted in center comes out clean. Cool 10 minutes. Loosen sides of loaves from pans; remove from pans to wire rack. Cool completely before slicing. Wrap tightly and store at room temperature up to 4 days, or refrigerate up to 10 days.

1 Slice:		% Daily Value:	
Calories	60	Vitamin A	0%
Calories from fat	0	Vitamin C	0%
Fat, g	0	Calcium	0%
Saturated, g	0	Iron	2%
Cholesterol, mg	0	**Diet Exchanges:**	
Sodium, mg	110	Starch/Bread	1
Carbohydrate, g	14		
Dietary Fiber, g	0		
Protein, g	1		

Southern Buttermilk Corn Bread

12 SERVINGS

What would a bowl of chili be without corn bread? Try this low-fat version with your next bowl of red.

1 1/2 cups yellow or white cornmeal

1/2 cup all-purpose flour

1 1/2 cups fat-free buttermilk

2 tablespoons vegetable oil

2 teaspoons baking powder

1 teaspoon sugar

1 teaspoon salt

1/2 teaspoon baking soda

1/2 cup fat-free cholesterol-free egg product or 4 egg whites

Heat oven to 450°. Grease bottom and side of round pan, 9 × 1 1/2 inches, square pan, 8 × 8 × 2 inches, or 10-inch ovenproof skillet with shortening.

Mix all ingredients. Beat vigorously 30 seconds. Pour batter into pan. Bake round or square pan 25 to 30 minutes, skillet about 20 minutes, or until golden brown. Serve warm.

1 Serving:		% Daily Value:	
Calories	120	Vitamin A	0%
Calories from fat	25	Vitamin C	0%
Fat, g	3	Calcium	8%
Saturated, g	1	Iron	6%
Cholesterol, mg	0	**Diet Exchanges:**	
Sodium, mg	360	Starch/Bread	1 1/2
Carbohydrate, g	20		
Dietary Fiber, g	1		
Protein, g	4		

Blueberry Streusel Muffins

12 MUFFINS

▨ ◊ ♥

Everybody's favorite muffin gets a makeover on page 26.

Streusel Topping (right)

1 cup skim milk

1/4 cup unsweetened applesauce

2 tablespoons vegetable oil

1/2 teaspoon vanilla

1/4 cup fat-free cholesterol-free egg product or 2 egg whites

2 cups all-purpose flour

1/3 cup sugar

3 teaspoons baking powder

1/2 teaspoon salt

1 cup fresh or canned (drained) blueberries*

Heat oven to 400°. Grease bottoms only of 12 medium muffin cups, 2 1/2 × 1 1/4 inches, with shortening, or line with paper baking cups. Prepare Streusel Topping; set aside.

Beat milk, applesauce, oil, vanilla and egg product in large bowl. Stir in flour, sugar, baking powder and salt all at once just until flour is moistened (batter will be lumpy). Fold in blueberries. Divide batter evenly among muffin cups. Sprinkle each with about 2 teaspoons topping.

Bake 20 to 25 minutes or until golden brown. Immediately remove from pan to wire rack. Serve warm if desired.

STREUSEL TOPPING

2 tablespoons firm margarine**

1/4 cup all-purpose flour

2 tablespoons packed brown sugar

1/4 teaspoon ground cinnamon

Cut margarine into flour, brown sugar and cinnamon in medium bowl, using pastry blender or crisscrossing 2 knives, until crumbly.

*3/4 cup frozen (thawed and well drained) blueberries can be substituted for the fresh or canned blueberries.

**Do not use spreads or tub products.

1 Muffin:		% Daily Value:	
Calories	155	Vitamin A	4%
Calories from fat	35	Vitamin C	0%
Fat, g	4	Calcium	10%
Saturated, g	1	Iron	8%
Cholesterol, mg	0	**Diet Exchanges:**	
Sodium, mg	250	Starch/Bread	2
Carbohydrate, g	29		
Dietary Fiber, g	1		
Protein, g	2		

Bran-Date Muffins

12 MUFFINS

1/2 cup hot water

3/4 cup chopped dates

1 1/2 cups wheat bran

1 cup whole wheat flour

1 teaspoon baking powder

1/2 teaspoon baking soda

1/2 teaspoon salt

1/4 cup strained prunes (baby food)

2 tablespoons vegetable oil

1/4 cup fat-free cholesterol-free egg product
   or 2 egg whites

1 cup fat-free buttermilk

Heat oven to 400°. Grease bottoms only of 12 medium muffin cups, 2 1/2 × 1 1/4 inches, with shortening, or line with paper baking cups. Pour hot water over 1/4 cup of the dates; set aside. Mix wheat bran, flour, baking powder, baking soda and salt in large bowl.

Place date-water mixture, prunes, oil and egg product in blender or food processor. Cover and blend on medium speed about 1 minute or until smooth. Stir blended mixture and buttermilk into flour mixture just until flour is moistened (batter will be lumpy). Gently stir in remaining 1/2 cup dates. Divide batter evenly among muffin cups.

Bake 20 to 22 minutes or until toothpick inserted in center comes out clean. Cool muffins in pan 5 minutes; remove from pan to wire rack. Serve warm if desired.

1 Muffin:		% Daily Value:	
Calories	110	Vitamin A	0%
Calories from fat	25	Vitamin C	0%
Fat, g	3	Calcium	6%
Saturated, g	1	Iron	8%
Cholesterol, mg	0	**Diet Exchanges:**	
Sodium, mg	210	Starch/Bread	1
Carbohydrate, g	22	Fruit	1/2
Dietary Fiber, g	5		
Protein, g	4		

Banana Muffins

12 MUFFINS

1 1/2 cups mashed ripe bananas (3 large)

2 tablespoons vegetable oil

1/4 cup fat-free cholesterol-free egg product or 2 egg whites

1/3 cup sugar

2 cups Bisquick® Reduced Fat baking mix

1/2 cup raisins or chopped nuts, if desired

Heat oven to 400°. Grease bottoms only of 12 medium muffin cups, 2 1/2 × 1 1/4 inches, with shortening, or line with paper baking cups. Beat bananas, oil, egg product and sugar in large bowl until well blended. Stir in baking mix and raisins just until baking mix is moistened (batter will be lumpy).

Divide batter evenly among muffin cups. Bake about 15 minutes or until golden brown. Cool muffins in pan 5 minutes; remove from pan to wire rack. Serve warm if desired.

1 Muffin:		% Daily Value:	
Calories	145	Vitamin A	0%
Calories from fat	35	Vitamin C	2%
Fat, g	4	Calcium	2%
Saturated, g	1	Iron	4%
Cholesterol, mg	0	**Diet Exchanges:**	
Sodium, mg	230	Starch/Bread	1
Carbohydrate, g	26	Fruit	1/2
Dietary Fiber, g	1	Fat	1
Protein, g	2		

Sour Cream Biscuits

8 BISCUITS

Space biscuits about 1 inch apart on cookie sheet for crusty biscuits or with sides touching for softer ones.

2 tablespoons firm margarine or spread

1 3/4 cups all-purpose flour

2 1/2 teaspoons baking powder

1/4 teaspoon salt

1/2 cup reduced-fat sour cream

1/3 cup skim milk

Heat oven to 450°. Cut margarine into flour, baking powder and salt in large bowl, using pastry blender or crisscrossing 2 knives, until mixture looks like fine crumbs. Mix sour cream and milk until smooth; stir into flour mixture until dough leaves side of bowl.

Turn dough onto lightly floured surface. Knead lightly 10 times. Roll or pat 1/2 inch thick. Cut with floured 2 1/2-inch round cutter. Place on ungreased cookie sheet. Bake 10 to 12 minutes or until golden brown. Serve hot.

1 Biscuit:		% Daily Value:	
Calories	145	Vitamin A	6%
Calories from fat	35	Vitamin C	0%
Fat, g	4	Calcium	12%
Saturated, g	1	Iron	8%
Cholesterol, mg	5	**Diet Exchanges:**	
Sodium, mg	270	Starch/Bread	1 1/2
Carbohydrate, g	24		
Dietary Fiber, g	1		
Protein, g	4		

Buttermilk–Toasted Oat Scones

8 SCONES

Scones were originally cooked on a griddle, but today most are oven-baked. The dough can be patted into a circle and cut into wedges, as below, or cut out with biscuit or cookie cutters into shapes.

1/2 cup quick-cooking or old-fashioned oats

1/2 cup oat bran

3 tablespoons firm margarine or spread

1 cup all-purpose flour

1/4 cup packed brown sugar

1 1/2 teaspoons baking powder

1/4 teaspoon baking soda

1/4 teaspoon salt

1/2 cup chopped figs or prunes

1/4 cup fat-free cholesterol-free egg product or 2 egg whites

About 1/2 cup fat-free buttermilk

Heat oven to 350°. Spread oats and oat bran in ungreased rectangular pan, 13 × 9 × 2 inches. Bake 15 to 20 minutes, stirring occasionally, until light brown; cool.

Increase oven temperature to 400°. Cut margarine into flour, brown sugar, baking powder, baking soda and salt in large bowl, using pastry blender or crisscrossing 2 knives, until mixture looks like fine crumbs. Stir in oat mixture and figs. Stir in egg product and just enough buttermilk so dough leaves side of bowl and forms a ball.

Turn dough onto lightly floured surface. Knead lightly 10 times. Place on ungreased cookie sheet. Pat into 8-inch circle, using floured hands. Cut circle into 12 wedges with sharp knife dipped in flour; do not separate. Brush with buttermilk and sprinkle with oats if desired.

Bake 16 to 18 minutes or until golden brown. Immediately remove from cookie sheet; carefully separate wedges. Serve warm.

1 Scone:		% Daily Value:	
Calories	170	Vitamin A	6%
Calories from fat	45	Vitamin C	0%
Fat, g	5	Calcium	8%
Saturated, g	1	Iron	8%
Cholesterol, mg	0	**Diet Exchanges:**	
Sodium, mg	280	Starch/Bread	2
Carbohydrate, g	29		
Dietary Fiber, g	2		
Protein, g	4		

Bran-Date Muffins (page 154), Buttermilk–Toasted Oat Scone

Citrus-Currant Scones

12 SCONES

1/4 cup sugar

2 teaspoons grated lemon or orange peel

1 3/4 cups all-purpose flour

2 1/2 teaspoons baking powder

1/4 teaspoon salt

3 tablespoons firm margarine or spread

1/3 cup plain low-fat yogurt

1/2 cup fat-free cholesterol-free egg product
or 3 egg whites, slightly beaten

1/2 cup currants or raisins

Skim milk

Heat oven to 375°. Mix sugar and lemon peel; reserve 1 tablespoon. Mix remaining sugar mixture, the flour, baking powder and salt in large bowl. Cut in margarine, using pastry blender or criss-crossing 2 knives, until mixture looks like fine crumbs. Stir in yogurt, egg product and currants just until dough leaves side of bowl and forms a ball.

Turn dough onto lightly floured surface. Knead lightly 10 times. Place on ungreased cookie sheet. Pat into 8-inch circle, using floured hands. Cut circle into 12 wedges with sharp knife dipped in flour; do not separate. Brush with milk. Sprinkle with reserved sugar mixture.

Bake 18 to 20 minutes or until edges are light brown. Immediately remove from cookie sheet; carefully separate wedges. Serve warm.

1 Scone:		% Daily Value:	
Calories	130	Vitamin A	4%
Calories from fat	25	Vitamin C	0%
Fat, g	3	Calcium	8%
Saturated, g	1	Iron	6%
Cholesterol, mg	0	**Diet Exchanges:**	
Sodium, mg	200	Starch/Bread	1
Carbohydrate, g	24	Fruit	1/2
Dietary Fiber, g	1		
Protein, g	3		

Popovers

6 POPOVERS

Popovers are perceived as difficult to make and high in cholesterol. Wrong, on both counts. Try these and you'll wonder why you never made popovers before.

1 egg plus 2 egg whites

1 cup all-purpose flour*

1 cup skim milk

1/2 teaspoon salt

Heat oven to 450°. Generously grease 6-cup popover pan or 6 six-ounce custard cups with shortening. Beat eggs slightly in medium bowl. Beat in remaining ingredients just until smooth (do not overbeat). Fill cups about half full.

Bake 20 minutes. Reduce oven temperature to 350°. Bake about 20 minutes longer or until deep golden brown. Immediately remove from cups. Serve hot.

*Do not use self-rising flour in this recipe.

1 Popover:		% Daily Value:	
Calories	100	Vitamin A	4%
Calories from fat	10	Vitamin C	0%
Fat, g	1	Calcium	6%
Saturated, g	0	Iron	6%
Cholesterol, mg	35	**Diet Exchanges:**	
Sodium, mg	230	Starch/Bread	1
Carbohydrate, g	18		
Dietary Fiber, g	1		
Protein, g	6		

Whole Wheat Blueberry Waffles

12 FOUR-INCH WAFFLE SQUARES

1 cup whole wheat flour

1 cup all-purpose flour

2 cups fat-free buttermilk

1/2 cup cholesterol-free egg product or 3 egg whites

1 tablespoon sugar

3 tablespoons vegetable oil

2 teaspoons baking powder

1 teaspoon grated orange peel

1/4 teaspoon salt

1 cup fresh or frozen (thawed and drained) blueberries

Heat waffle iron; brush lightly with oil if necessary. Beat all ingredients except blueberries just until smooth. Stir in blueberries. Pour batter from cup or pitcher onto hot waffle iron. Bake about 5 minutes or until steaming stops. Carefully remove waffle.

1 Square:		% Daily Value:	
Calories	130	Vitamin A	0%
Calories from fat	35	Vitamin C	2%
Fat, g	4	Calcium	10%
Saturated, g	1	Iron	6%
Cholesterol, mg	2	**Diet Exchanges:**	
Sodium, mg	180	Starch/Bread	1
Carbohydrate, g	20	Fruit	1/2
Dietary Fiber, g	2		
Protein, g	5		

Apple-Noodle Kugel

8 SERVINGS

Serve this noodle side dish with Garlicky Pork with Basil (page 68) or Meat Loaf (page 54) and steamed fresh vegetables sprinkled with a little seasoned pepper.

6 cups cooked cholesterol-free wide noodles

1 large tart apple, thinly sliced (1 1/2 cups)

1/2 cup raisins or other chopped dried fruit

1 container (8 ounces) fat-free cholesterol-free egg product (1 cup)

1 cup fat-free cottage cheese

1/2 cup vanilla low-fat yogurt

1/4 cup honey or sugar

2 tablespoons skim milk

1 teaspoon cornstarch

1 teaspoon ground cinnamon

Heat oven to 350°. Spray rectangular pan, 13 × 9 × 2 inches, with nonstick cooking spray. Spread noodles in pan. Top with apple and raisins.

Place remaining ingredients in blender or food processor. Cover and blend on medium speed until blended; pour over noodles. Bake uncovered about 1 hour or until light brown and center is set.

1 Serving:		% Daily Value:	
Calories	280	Vitamin A	4%
Calories from fat	20	Vitamin C	0%
Fat, g	2	Calcium	8%
Saturated, g	1	Iron	16%
Cholesterol, mg	0	**Diet Exchanges:**	
Sodium, mg	160	Starch/Bread	3
Carbohydrate, g	55	Fruit	1/2
Dietary Fiber, g	3		
Protein, g	13		

Spanish Gazpacho Rice

4 SERVINGS (3/4 CUP EACH)

1/2 cup fat-free chicken broth

3 medium onions, chopped (1 1/2 cups)

3 cloves garlic, finely chopped

2 cups sliced mushrooms (6 ounces)

1 medium red bell pepper, diced (1 cup)

2 cups cooked rice

1 cup frozen green peas

2 tablespoons chopped fresh parsley

1 tablespoon chopped fresh cilantro

1/4 teaspoon salt

1 can (16 ounces) whole peeled tomatoes, undrained

Heat broth to boiling in Dutch oven over medium-high heat. Cook onions, garlic, mushrooms and bell pepper in broth 5 to 8 minutes, stirring frequently, until vegetables are crisp-tender.

Stir in remaining ingredients, breaking up tomatoes. Cook 5 to 8 minutes, stirring frequently, until vegetables are tender and liquid is absorbed.

1 Serving:		% Daily Value:	
Calories	175	Vitamin A	20%
Calories from fat	10	Vitamin C	52%
Fat, g	1	Calcium	6%
Saturated, g	0	Iron	16%
Cholesterol, mg	0	**Diet Exchanges:**	
Sodium, mg	450	Starch/Bread	2
Carbohydrate, g	40	Vegetable	2
Dietary Fiber, g	5		
Protein, g	7		

Cumin Confetti Rice

4 SERVINGS (3/4 CUP EACH)

1/2 cup fat-free chicken broth or vegetable broth

3 cloves garlic, finely chopped

1 cup chopped green onions (9 medium)

1 medium green bell pepper, diced (1 cup)

1 medium red bell pepper, diced (1 cup)

1/4 cup shredded carrot

2 cups cooked brown or basmati rice

1/4 teaspoon ground cumin

1 teaspoon soy sauce

Heat broth to boiling in 10-inch nonstick skillet over medium-high heat. Cook garlic, onions and bell peppers in broth 5 to 8 minutes, stirring frequently, until bell pepper is tender. Stir in remaining ingredients; heat through.

1 Serving:		% Daily Value:	
Calories	130	Vitamin A	26%
Calories from fat	10	Vitamin C	62%
Fat, g	1	Calcium	4%
Saturated, g	0	Iron	6%
Cholesterol, mg	0	**Diet Exchanges:**	
Sodium, mg	200	Starch/Bread	2
Carbohydrate, g	29		
Dietary Fiber, g	3		
Protein, g	4		

"Fried" Wild Rice with Corn

4 SERVINGS (ABOUT 1 CUP EACH)

This rice, of course, is not fried at all, but if you don't tell, we won't.

1/2 cup fat-free chicken broth

1/2 cup chopped green onions (5 medium)

2 cloves garlic, finely chopped

1/2 cup sliced mushrooms (1 1/2 ounces)

1/4 cup shredded carrot

1 cup frozen whole kernel corn

3 cups cooked wild rice

1 tablespoon soy sauce

1/8 teaspoon pepper

Chopped green onion, if desired

Heat broth to boiling in 10-inch nonstick skillet over medium-high heat. Cook 1/2 cup onions, the garlic, mushrooms and carrot in broth 5 to 8 minutes, stirring frequently, until vegetables are crisp-tender.

Stir in corn and wild rice. Cook 3 minutes, stirring constantly (mixture will be dry). Stir in soy sauce and pepper; heat through. Sprinkle with onion.

1 Serving:		% Daily Value:	
Calories	175	Vitamin A	12%
Calories from fat	10	Vitamin C	4%
Fat, g	1	Calcium	2%
Saturated, g	0	Iron	8%
Cholesterol, mg	0	**Diet Exchanges:**	
Sodium, mg	360	Starch/Bread	2
Carbohydrate, g	37	Vegetable	1
Dietary Fiber, g	3		
Protein, g	7		

"Fried" Wild Rice with Corn, Cumin Confetti Rice (page 161)

Sweet Potato Risotto

4 SERVINGS (3/4 CUP EACH)

Sweet potato adds a new twist to the growing popularity of risotto.

2 tablespoons dry white wine or water

1/3 cup chopped onion

1 clove garlic, finely chopped

1 cup uncooked arborio or other short-grain white rice

1/2 cup mashed cooked sweet potato

3 3/4 cups fat-free chicken broth or vegetable broth, warmed

2 tablespoons grated reduced-fat Parmesan cheese blend

1/2 teaspoon chopped fresh or 1/4 teaspoon dried rosemary leaves

1/8 teaspoon ground nutmeg

1/8 teaspoon salt

Spray 3-quart nonstick saucepan with nonstick cooking spray. Heat wine to boiling in saucepan over medium-high heat. Cook onion and garlic in wine 3 to 4 minutes, stirring frequently, until onion is tender. Stir in rice. Cook 1 minute, stirring constantly.

Stir in sweet potato and 1/2 cup of the broth. Cook, stirring constantly, until liquid is completely absorbed. Stir in an additional 1/2 cup broth. Continue cooking about 20 minutes, adding broth 1/2 cup at a time after previous additions have been absorbed and stirring constantly, until rice is creamy and just tender; remove from heat. Stir in remaining ingredients.

1 Serving:		% Daily Value:	
Calories	130	Vitamin A	22%
Calories from fat	20	Vitamin C	4%
Fat, g	2	Calcium	6%
Saturated, g	1	Iron	8%
Cholesterol, mg	2	**Diet Exchanges:**	
Sodium, mg	860	Starch/Bread	1
Carbohydrate, g	22	Vegetable	1
Dietary Fiber, g	1		
Protein, g	7		

Buttery Herb Couscous

4 SERVINGS (1/2 CUP EACH)

2 teaspoons margarine or spread

2 cloves garlic, finely chopped

1 green onion, chopped

2/3 cup uncooked couscous

1 1/3 cups fat-free chicken broth or vegetable broth

1/4 teaspoon salt

2 teaspoons finely chopped fresh or 1 teaspoon dried basil leaves

1 teaspoon finely chopped fresh or 1/4 teaspoon dried thyme leaves

2 tablespoons grated reduced-fat Parmesan cheese blend

Melt margarine in 2-quart nonstick saucepan over medium heat. Cook garlic and onion in margarine 1 minute, stirring constantly. Stir in couscous. Stir in broth and salt. Heat to boiling; remove from heat. Cover and let stand 5 minutes. Stir in basil, thyme and cheese.

1 Serving:		% Daily Value:	
Calories	150	Vitamin A	2%
Calories from fat	25	Vitamin C	0%
Fat, g	3	Calcium	4%
Saturated, g	1	Iron	4%
Cholesterol, mg	2	**Diet Exchanges:**	
Sodium, mg	460	Starch/Bread	1 1/2
Carbohydrate, g	25		
Dietary Fiber, g	1		
Protein, g	7		

Sweet Potato–Apple Puree

4 SERVINGS (ABOUT 2/3 CUP EACH)

Because yams are darker than sweet potatoes, they give this puree a more intense color. Try piping this puree into individual servings.

3 medium sweet potatoes or yams, peeled and cubed (3 cups)

2 medium cooking apples, peeled and coarsely chopped (2 cups)

1 tablespoon apple brandy, if desired

1/8 teaspoon salt

Heat 1/2 inch water to boiling in 3-quart saucepan. Add sweet potatoes and apples. Cover and heat to boiling; reduce heat. Boil 8 to 10 minutes or until tender; drain. Add brandy and salt; mash.

1 Serving:		% Daily Value:	
Calories	110	Vitamin A	100%
Calories from fat	0	Vitamin C	18%
Fat, g	0	Calcium	2%
Saturated, g	0	Iron	2%
Cholesterol, mg	0	**Diet Exchanges:**	
Sodium, mg	80	Vegetable	1
Carbohydrate, g	30	Fruit	1 1/2
Dietary Fiber, g	3		
Protein, g	1		

Beets in Sweet Orange Sauce

4 SERVINGS (ABOUT 1/2 CUP EACH)

Fresh beets are a wonderful treat few people take time to prepare. First baked and then glazed, these beets will get you requests for a repeat performance.

1 bunch beets (4 to 5 medium)

1 teaspoon olive or vegetable oil

1/4 cup fat-free chicken broth

1/3 cup orange juice

1 teaspoon grated orange peel

2 tablespoons packed brown sugar

3 tablespoons chopped fresh parsley

**1/2 teaspoon chopped crystallized ginger or
    1/4 teaspoon ground ginger**

Heat oven to 400°. Cut beets into fourths. Place beets, oil and broth in ovenproof 2-quart saucepan. Cover and bake 30 to 45 minutes, stirring occasionally, until beets are tender. Remove from oven.

Stir in orange juice, orange peel and brown sugar. Cook over medium-high heat 5 to 8 minutes, stirring frequently, until sauce is reduced and beets are coated with glaze. Stir in parsley and ginger.

1 Serving:		% Daily Value:	
Calories	75	Vitamin A	2%
Calories from fat	10	Vitamin C	12%
Fat, g	1	Calcium	2%
Saturated, g	0	Iron	6%
Cholesterol, mg	0	**Diet Exchanges:**	
Sodium, mg	115	Vegetable	2
Carbohydrate, g	17	Fruit	1/2
Dietary Fiber, g	2		
Protein, g	2		

*Beets in Sweet Orange Sauce, Parmesan-Basil Perch
(page 100)*

Leeks au Gratin

4 SERVINGS (ABOUT 1/2 CUP EACH)

4 medium leeks with tops (2 pounds), cut into 1/2-inch pieces

Crumb Topping (right)

1 tablespoon margarine or spread

1 tablespoon plus 1 teaspoon all-purpose flour

1/4 teaspoon salt

Dash of pepper

2/3 cup skim milk

1/2 cup shredded Gruyère cheese (2 ounces)

Heat 1 inch water to boiling in 3-quart saucepan. Add leeks. Cover and cook over medium heat about 5 minutes or until crisp-tender; drain. Prepare Crumb Topping.

Heat oven to 325°. Spray shallow 1-quart casserole with nonstick cooking spray. Melt margarine in 2-quart saucepan over low heat. Stir in flour, salt and pepper. Cook over low heat, stirring constantly, until margarine is absorbed; remove from heat. Gradually stir in milk. Heat to boiling, stirring constantly. Boil and stir 1 minute. Stir in cheese until melted.

Stir in leeks. Pour into casserole. Sprinkle with topping. Bake uncovered about 25 minutes or until heated through.

CRUMB TOPPING

2 tablespoons dry bread crumbs

1 teaspoon margarine or spread, melted

Mix ingredients.

1 Serving:		% Daily Value:	
Calories	145	Vitamin A	12%
Calories from fat	70	Vitamin C	14%
Fat, g	8	Calcium	24%
Saturated, g	3	Iron	8%
Cholesterol, mg	15	**Diet Exchanges:**	
Sodium, mg	280	Vegetable	1
Carbohydrate, g	13	Skim milk	1/2
Dietary Fiber, g	2	Fat	1
Protein, g	7		

Tangy Carrots with Grapes

4 SERVINGS (ABOUT 1/2 CUP EACH)

**4 medium carrots, cut into thin diagonal
  slices (2 cups)**

1 shallot, chopped

1/4 cup water

2 tablespoons balsamic or red wine vinegar

1 tablespoon packed brown sugar

1/2 cup seedless grape halves

Heat water to boiling in 10-inch nonstick skillet over medium heat. Cook carrots and shallot in water 8 to 10 minutes, stirring frequently, until water has evaporated and carrots are tender.

Push carrot mixture to side of skillet. Mix vinegar and brown sugar in other side of skillet. Add grapes. Toss carrot mixture, grapes and vinegar mixture.

1 Serving:		% Daily Value:	
Calories	55	Vitamin A	100%
Calories from fat	0	Vitamin C	8%
Fat, g	0	Calcium	2%
Saturated, g	0	Iron	2%
Cholesterol, mg	0	**Diet Exchanges:**	
Sodium, mg	25	Vegetable	1
Carbohydrate, g	15	Fruit	1/2
Dietary Fiber, g	2		
Protein, g	1		

Sweet-Sour Cabbage with Plantain

4 SERVINGS (ABOUT 3/4 CUP EACH)

Plantains are ripe when their skins turn black and they are slightly soft. A firm medium banana can be used if plantain isn't available.

1/4 cup fat-free chicken broth

2 tablespoons packed brown sugar

2 tablespoons cider vinegar

2 teaspoons cornstarch

1/4 teaspoon red pepper sauce

2 teaspoons vegetable oil

**1 ripe medium plantain, cut into 1/4-inch
  slices**

1/3 cup sliced green onions (4 medium)

1/4 cup 1 × 1/8-inch strips red bell pepper

**1 small head savoy cabbage, coarsely
  shredded (4 cups)**

Mix broth, brown sugar, vinegar, cornstarch and pepper sauce; set aside. Heat oil in 10-inch nonstick skillet over high heat. Add plantain, onions and bell pepper; stir-fry 1 minute. Add cabbage; stir-fry 2 minutes. Stir in cornstarch mixture; cook and stir about 10 seconds or until thickened.

1 Serving:		% Daily Value:	
Calories	155	Vitamin A	10%
Calories from fat	25	Vitamin C	34%
Fat, g	3	Calcium	4%
Saturated, g	0	Iron	6%
Cholesterol, mg	0	**Diet Exchanges:**	
Sodium, mg	70	Starch/Bread	1
Carbohydrate, g	32	Vegetable	1
Dietary Fiber, g	2	Fruit	1
Protein, g	2		

Three-Pepper Stir-fry

4 SERVINGS (ABOUT 1/2 CUP EACH)

3/4 cup fat-free chicken broth

2 teaspoons grated gingerroot

2 cloves garlic, finely chopped

1 medium red bell pepper, thinly sliced

1 medium yellow bell pepper, thinly sliced

1 medium orange or green bell pepper, thinly sliced

1 tablespoon hoisin sauce

Heat half of the broth to boiling in nonstick wok or 10-inch skillet over medium-high heat. Add gingerroot and garlic; stir-fry 1 minute. Add bell peppers and remaining broth. Cook 5 to 8 minutes, stirring occasionally, until vegetables are tender and most of liquid has evaporated. Stir in hoisin sauce.

1 Serving:		% Daily Value:	
Calories	35	Vitamin A	32%
Calories from fat	10	Vitamin C	90%
Fat, g	1	Calcium	0%
Saturated, g	0	Iron	2%
Cholesterol, mg	0	**Diet Exchanges:**	
Sodium, mg	150	Vegetable	1
Carbohydrate, g	6		
Dietary Fiber, g	1		
Protein, g	2		

Oriental Coleslaw

4 SERVINGS (ABOUT 3/4 CUP EACH)

2 cups finely shredded napa (Chinese) cabbage (8 ounces)

1/4 cup chopped jicama

1/4 cup chopped green bell pepper

1/4 cup coarsely shredded carrot

Sesame Dressing (below)

Toss all ingredients.

SESAME DRESSING

3 tablespoons rice vinegar or white wine vinegar

2 teaspoons sugar

2 teaspoons sesame seed, toasted

2 teaspoons reduced-sodium soy sauce

1 teaspoon sesame oil

1/8 teaspoon crushed red pepper

Mix all ingredients.

1 Serving:		% Daily Value:	
Calories	40	Vitamin A	22%
Calories from fat	20	Vitamin C	38%
Fat, g	2	Calcium	4%
Saturated, g	0	Iron	2%
Cholesterol, mg	0	**Diet Exchanges:**	
Sodium, mg	130	Vegetable	1
Carbohydrate, g	6		
Dietary Fiber, g	1		
Protein, g	1		

Zesty Fruit Salad

4 SERVINGS (ABOUT 1 CUP EACH)

1 cup strawberries, cut in half

1 medium papaya, peeled, seeded and cut
 into 1-inch pieces (2 cups)

1 kiwifruit, peeled and thinly sliced

1 starfruit, thinly sliced and seeded

Jalapeño Dressing (below)

Toss all ingredients. Serve on salad greens if
desired.

JALAPEÑO DRESSING

1 tablespoon chopped fresh cilantro

1 tablespoon vegetable oil

1 tablespoon lime juice

1 teaspoon sugar

1/2 small jalapeño chili, seeded and very
 finely chopped

Mix all ingredients.

1 Serving:		% Daily Value:	
Calories	90	Vitamin A	8%
Calories from fat	35	Vitamin C	100%
Fat, g	4	Calcium	2%
Saturated, g	1	Iron	2%
Cholesterol, mg	0	**Diet Exchanges:**	
Sodium, mg	5	Fruit	1
Carbohydrate, g	16	Fat	1
Dietary Fiber, g	3		
Protein, g	1		

Two-Potato Salad with Dill Dressing

4 SERVINGS (ABOUT 1 CUP EACH)

1/2 cup plain fat-free yogurt

1 tablespoon fat-free mayonnaise or salad
 dressing

1 teaspoon chopped fresh or 1/2 teaspoon
 dried dill weed

1 teaspoon Dijon mustard

1/4 teaspoon salt

2 cups cubed cooked white potato (1 large)

2 cups cubed cooked sweet potato (1 large)

1 small stalk celery, chopped (1/3 cup)

1/4 cup sliced radishes

2 tablespoons chopped green onions

Mix yogurt, mayonnaise, dill weed, mustard and
salt in large glass or plastic bowl. Add remaining
ingredients; toss. Cover and refrigerate about
4 hours or until chilled.

1 Serving:		% Daily Value:	
Calories	95	Vitamin A	98%
Calories from fat	0	Vitamin C	30%
Fat, g	0	Calcium	8%
Saturated, g	0	Iron	2%
Cholesterol, mg	0	**Diet Exchanges:**	
Sodium, mg	240	Starch/Bread	1
Carbohydrate, g	23	Vegetable	1
Dietary Fiber, g	2		
Protein, g	3		

Fat-free Salad Dressings

We have developed four fat-free salad dressings using flavorful ingredients so you won't miss the fat. Peppercorns, cilantro, herbs, chutney, curry, apple juice and horseradish are but a few of the tantalizing flavors lying in wait for your sampling.

RASPBERRY-CILANTRO DRESSING

ABOUT **1** CUP DRESSING

1 tablespoon sugar

2 teaspoons cornstarch

1/8 teaspoon salt

2/3 cup water

1/3 cup raspberry vinegar

1 tablespoon chopped fresh cilantro

Mix sugar, cornstarch and salt in 1-quart saucepan. Gradually stir in water and vinegar. Cook stirring constantly, until mixture thickens and boils. Boil and stir 1 minute; remove from heat. Stir in cilantro. Cover and refrigerate any remaining dressing.

2 Tablespoons:		% Daily Value:	
Calories	10	Vitamin A	0%
Calories from fat	0	Vitamin C	0%
Fat, g	0	Calcium	0%
Saturated, g	0	Iron	0%
Cholesterol, mg	0	**Diet Exchanges:**	
Sodium, mg	35	Free food	
Carbohydrate, g	3		
Dietary Fiber, g	0		
Protein, g	0		

CREAMY HERB DRESSING

ABOUT **2** CUPS DRESSING

1 cup plain fat-free yogurt

1/4 cup fat-free mayonnaise

3/4 cup fat-free buttermilk

2 tablespoons chopped green onions

1 tablespoon chopped fresh parsley

1/2 teaspoon dried dill weed

1/2 teaspoon Worcestershire sauce

1/4 teaspoon salt

1 clove garlic, finely chopped

Dash of freshly ground pepper

Mix all ingredients. Cover and refrigerate any remaining dressing.

2 Tablespoons:		% Daily Value:	
Calories	15	Vitamin A	0%
Calories from fat	0	Vitamin C	0%
Fat, g	0	Calcium	4%
Saturated, g	0	Iron	0%
Cholesterol, mg	0	**Diet Exchanges:**	
Sodium, mg	105	Free food	
Carbohydrate, g	3		
Dietary Fiber, g	0		
Protein, g	1		

CURRIED YOGURT DRESSING

ABOUT 1 CUP DRESSING

1 cup plain fat-free yogurt

1 tablespoon mango chutney, chopped

1 teaspoon curry powder

1/2 teaspoon salt

Mix all ingredients. Cover and refrigerate any remaining dressing.

2 Tablespoons:		% Daily Value:	
Calories	20	Vitamin A	0%
Calories from fat	0	Vitamin C	0%
Fat, g	0	Calcium	6%
Saturated, g	0	Iron	0%
Cholesterol, mg	0	**Diet Exchanges:**	
Sodium, mg	160	Free food	
Carbohydrate, g	3		
Dietary Fiber, g	0		
Protein, g	2		

APPLE-HORSERADISH DRESSING

ABOUT 3/4 CUP DRESSING

1/4 cup water

1/4 cup frozen (thawed) apple juice concentrate

2 tablespoons chopped fresh parsley

2 tablespoons finely shredded apple

2 tablespoons cider vinegar

1 teaspoon prepared horseradish

1/4 teaspoon salt

1/8 teaspoon pepper

Mix all ingredients with fork or wire whisk.

2 Tablespoons:		% Daily Value:	
Calories	20	Vitamin A	0%
Calories from fat	0	Vitamin C	4%
Fat, g	0	Calcium	0%
Saturated, g	0	Iron	2%
Cholesterol, mg	0	**Diet Exchanges:**	
Sodium, mg	90	Vegetable	1
Carbohydrate, g	5		
Dietary Fiber, g	0		
Protein, g	0		

173

Warm Greens with Balsamic Vinaigrette

4 SERVINGS (ABOUT 1 CUP EACH)

The characteristically rich flavor and aroma of Italian balsamic vinegar are due, in part, to aging in wooden casks for several months. Use the remaining vinaigrette as you would any salad dressing.

1/4 cup Balsamic Vinaigrette (right)

1 1/2 cups sliced mushrooms (4 ounces)

2 cups 2-inch pieces leaf lettuce

2 cups 2-inch pieces spinach

1 1/2 cups 2-inch pieces radicchio

2 tablespoons pine nuts, toasted

Heat Balsamic Vinaigrette to boiling in 10-inch nonstick skillet over medium heat. Cook mushrooms in vinaigrette 3 minutes; remove from heat. Add remaining ingredients. Toss 1 to 2 minutes or until greens begin to wilt. Serve immediately. Sprinkle with freshly ground pepper if desired.

BALSAMIC VINAIGRETTE

ABOUT **1** CUP DRESSING

1/3 cup water

1/4 cup balsamic vinegar

1/4 cup olive or vegetable oil

1 teaspoon honey

1/4 teaspoon salt

1/4 teaspoon paprika

1 clove garlic, finely chopped

Shake all ingredients in tightly covered container.

1 Serving:		% Daily Value:	
Calories	75	Vitamin A	30%
Calories from fat	54	Vitamin C	26%
Fat, g	6	Calcium	4%
Saturated, g	1	Iron	8%
Cholesterol, mg	0	**Diet Exchanges:**	
Sodium, mg	65	Vegetable	1
Carbohydrate, g	5		
Dietary Fiber, g	2		
Protein, g	2		

Warm Greens with Balsamic Vinaigrette

Orange Béarnaise Sauce

ABOUT 1 CUP SAUCE

Serve this delicious mock béarnaise with chicken, fish or beef. It is thickened with cornstarch rather than egg yolks.

1/2 cup cold water

1 tablespoon cornstarch

1/4 cup margarine or spread

1/2 teaspoon grated orange peel

1 tablespoon orange juice

1 tablespoon finely chopped onion

1 teaspoon chopped fresh or 1/4 teaspoon dried chervil leaves

1 teaspoon chopped fresh or 1/4 teaspoon dried tarragon leaves

1/8 teaspoon salt

3 drops yellow food color, if desired

1/3 cup plain fat-free yogurt

Gradually stir cold water into cornstarch in 1-quart nonstick saucepan. Stir in remaining ingredients except yogurt. Heat over medium heat, stirring constantly, until mixture thickens and boils. Boil and stir 1 minute; remove from heat.

Place yogurt in small bowl. Beat vigorously with fork until smooth. Pour hot mixture into yogurt, beating constantly with fork.

2 Tablespoons:		% Daily Value:	
Calories	65	Vitamin A	8%
Calories from fat	55	Vitamin C	0%
Fat, g	6	Calcium	2%
Saturated, g	1	Iron	0%
Cholesterol, mg	0	**Diet Exchanges:**	
Sodium, mg	110	Fat	1
Carbohydrate, g	2		
Dietary Fiber, g	0		
Protein, g	1		

Tartar Sauce

ABOUT 1 1/4 CUPS SAUCE

This reduced-fat tartar sauce is a wonderful accompaniment to fish, of course, but makes a great sandwich spread, too.

1 cup fat-free mayonnaise or salad dressing

1/4 cup finely chopped dill pickle

1 tablespoon chopped fresh parsley

1 tablespoon chopped green onion

2 teaspoons lemon juice

1/2 teaspoon Dijon mustard

Mix all ingredients. Cover and refrigerate about 1 hour or until chilled.

2 Tablespoons:		% Daily Value:	
Calories	20	Vitamin A	0%
Calories from fat	0	Vitamin C	2%
Fat, g	0	Calcium	0%
Saturated, g	0	Iron	0%
Cholesterol, mg	0	**Diet Exchanges:**	
Sodium, mg	350	Vegetable	1
Carbohydrate, g	5		
Dietary Fiber, g	0		
Protein, g	0		

Orange Béarnaise Sauce

White Sauce

ABOUT 1 CUP SAUCE

This variation of classic white sauce, made with skim milk and half the usual amount of margarine, is a fine substitute.

1 tablespoon margarine or spread

2 tablespoons all-purpose flour

1/4 teaspoon salt

1/8 teaspoon pepper

1 cup skim milk

Melt margarine in 1 1/2-quart nonstick saucepan over low heat. Stir in flour, salt and pepper. Cook over low heat, stirring constantly, until margarine is absorbed; remove from heat. Gradually stir in milk. Heat to boiling, stirring constantly. Boil and stir 1 minute.

2 Tablespoons:		% Daily Value:	
Calories	35	Vitamin A	4%
Calories from fat	20	Vitamin C	0%
Fat, g	2	Calcium	4%
Saturated, g	0	Iron	0%
Cholesterol, mg	0	**Diet Exchanges:**	
Sodium, mg	100	Vegetable	1
Carbohydrate, g	3		
Dietary Fiber, g	0		
Protein, g	1		

Mushroom Sauce

ABOUT 1 1/4 CUPS SAUCE

1 tablespoon margarine or spread

**1/2 cup thinly sliced mushrooms
(1 1/2 ounces)**

2 tablespoons all-purpose flour

**1/2 teaspoon chopped fresh or 1/4 teaspoon
dried tarragon leaves**

1/4 teaspoon salt

1/8 teaspoon pepper

1 cup skim milk

1 tablespoon dry sherry, if desired

Melt margarine in 1 1/2-quart nonstick saucepan over medium-high heat. Cook mushrooms in margarine, stirring frequently, until liquid has evaporated.

Stir in flour, tarragon, salt and pepper. Cook over low heat, stirring constantly, until margarine is absorbed; remove from heat. Gradually stir in milk. Heat to boiling, stirring constantly. Boil and stir 2 minutes. Stir in sherry.

2 Tablespoons:		% Daily Value:	
Calories	25	Vitamin A	2%
Calories from fat	10	Vitamin C	0%
Fat, g	1	Calcium	2%
Saturated, g	0	Iron	0%
Cholesterol, mg	0	**Diet Exchanges:**	
Sodium, mg	80	Vegetable	1
Carbohydrate, g	3		
Dietary Fiber, g	0		
Protein, g	1		

Cucumber-Yogurt Sauce

ABOUT 1 1/4 CUPS SAUCE

1 large cucumber, peeled, seeded, shredded and drained

1/2 cup plain fat-free yogurt

1 tablespoon chopped fresh or 1 teaspoon dried dill weed

1 1/2 teaspoons chopped fresh mint leaves

1/2 teaspoon Dijon mustard

1/8 teaspoon salt

Mix all ingredients. Cover and refrigerate about 1 hour or until chilled.

2 Tablespoons:		% Daily Value:	
Calories	10	Vitamin A	0%
Calories from fat	0	Vitamin C	2%
Fat, g	0	Calcium	2%
Saturated, g	0	Iron	0%
Cholesterol, mg	0	**Diet Exchanges:**	
Sodium, mg	40	Free food	
Carbohydrate, g	2		
Dietary Fiber, g	0		
Protein, g	1		

Pineapple Salsa

ABOUT 2 1/2 CUPS SALSA

This flavorful fat-free salsa tops Tropical Mahimahi (page 96), but would also go great with grilled chicken.

1 small red bell pepper, finely chopped (1/2 cup)

1 small red onion, finely chopped (1/4 cup)

1 small red chili, seeded and finely chopped

2 cups 1/2-inch pieces pineapple (1/2 medium)

2 tablespoons chopped fresh cilantro

2 tablespoons lime juice

Cook bell pepper, onion and chili in 8-inch nonstick skillet over medium heat, stirring frequently, until tender. Stir in remaining ingredients. Cover and refrigerate about 2 hours or until chilled.

2 Tablespoons:		% Daily Value:	
Calories	10	Vitamin A	4%
Calories from fat	0	Vitamin C	8%
Fat, g	0	Calcium	0%
Saturated, g	0	Iron	0%
Cholesterol, mg	0	**Diet Exchanges:**	
Sodium, mg	0	Free food	
Carbohydrate, g	3		
Dietary Fiber, g	0		
Protein, g	0		

Sweet Pepper Relish

ABOUT **1 1/4** CUPS RELISH

1 medium red bell pepper

1 medium yellow bell pepper

1 medium green bell pepper

2 tablespoons pine nuts, toasted

1 tablespoon chopped fresh or 1 teaspoon
dried basil leaves

1 tablespoon red wine vinegar

1/4 teaspoon salt

2 cloves garlic, finely chopped

Set oven control to broil. Place bell peppers on rack in broiler pan. Broil with tops about 5 inches from heat 12 to 16 minutes, turning occasionally, until skin is blistered and evenly browned. Place peppers in plastic bag; close tightly. Let stand 15 to 20 minutes.

Peel peppers; remove stems, seeds and membranes. Chop peppers. Mix peppers and remaining ingredients. Cover and refrigerate at least 1 hour to blend flavors.

2 Tablespoons:		% Daily Value:	
Calories	15	Vitamin A	8%
Calories from fat	10	Vitamin C	28%
Fat, g	1	Calcium	0%
Saturated, g	0	Iron	0%
Cholesterol, mg	0	**Diet Exchanges:**	
Sodium, mg	55	Free food	
Carbohydrate, g	2		
Dietary Fiber, g	0		
Protein, g	0		

Sweet Pepper Relish on Tropical Mahimahi (page 96),
Cucumber-Yogurt Sauce (page 179), Pineapple Salsa
(page 179), Tartar Sauce (page 176)

7

Delicious Desserts

- Satisfying desserts don't always have to be gooey. Enjoy fresh fruits chopped, pureed, cold, hot, with sauces or without. Always use ripe fruit for the most flavorful results.

- Take advantage of the reduced-fat and fat-free dairy products available today to substitute in your favorite recipes.

- Angel food cake is a perfect dessert for the low-fat, low-cholesterol crowd. It can be as simple as a slice topped with fresh fruit or try it stuffed with sherbet (page 186) or cut up in a trifle (page 190).

- From top to bottom, meringues make for a nearly guilt-free dessert. Try it as a frosting (page 188) or as a base (page 194).

Chocolate Swirl Cheesecake with Raspberry Topping (page 185)

Broiled Pineapple

4 SERVINGS (3 SLICES PINEAPPLE AND 2 TABLE-SPOONS SAUCE EACH)

This recipe is so simple using canned pineapple, but twelve 3/8-inch slices of fresh pineapple can be used instead.

1 can (20 ounces) sliced pineapple in juice, drained

1 tablespoon packed brown sugar

2 tablespoons lime juice

2 tablespoons honey

1/2 cup vanilla fat-free yogurt

1 teaspoon honey

1/2 teaspoon grated lime peel

Set oven control to broil. Place pineapple slices in ungreased broiler pan. Mix brown sugar, lime juice and 2 tablespoons honey; drizzle over pineapple. Broil with tops of pineapple 4 inches from heat 6 to 8 minutes, turning once, until light brown.

Mix remaining ingredients. Place 3 slices pineapple on each of 4 dessert plates. Spoon yogurt mixture over pineapple.

1 Serving:		% Daily Value:	
Calories	145	Vitamin A	2%
Calories from fat	0	Vitamin C	20%
Fat, g	0	Calcium	6%
Saturated, g	0	Iron	4%
Cholesterol, mg	0	**Diet Exchanges:**	
Sodium, mg	15	Fruit	2
Carbohydrate, g	34		
Dietary Fiber, g	1		
Protein, g	2		

Grilled Peaches with Blackberry Sauce

4 SERVINGS (2 PEACH HALVES AND 1/4 CUP SAUCE EACH)

2 cups frozen blackberries

1/2 teaspoon lime juice

1 tablespoon honey, packed brown sugar or maple syrup

4 medium peaches, cut in half and pitted*

1 1/2 tablespoons packed brown sugar

1/2 teaspoon ground cinnamon

1 teaspoon peach liqueur or lime juice

Place blackberries, lime juice and honey in blender. Cover and blend on medium speed about 45 seconds, stopping blender occasionally to scrape sides, until smooth. Strain sauce. Cover and refrigerate until serving time.

Heat grill or set oven control to broil. Place peach halves, cut sides up, on large piece of heavy-duty aluminum foil. Sprinkle with brown sugar, cinnamon and liqueur. Fold foil over peaches and seal. Place on grill over medium-hot coals or under broiler about 4 inches from heat. Grill or broil about 15 minutes or until heated through. Serve hot with blackberry sauce.

*8 canned peach halves, in their own juice, can be substituted for the fresh peaches.

1 Serving:		% Daily Value:	
Calories	125	Vitamin A	4%
Calories from fat	0	Vitamin C	24%
Fat, g	0	Calcium	2%
Saturated, g	0	Iron	2%
Cholesterol, mg	0	**Diet Exchanges:**	
Sodium, mg	2	Fruit	2
Carbohydrate, g	30		
Dietary Fiber, g	3		
Protein, g	1		

Chocolate Swirl Cheesecake with Raspberry Topping

12 SERVINGS (WITH ABOUT 2 TABLESPOONS SAUCE EACH)

4 chocolate wafers, crushed (1/4 cup)

2 cups Thick Yogurt (page 32)

1 package (8 ounces) reduced-fat cream cheese (Neufchâtel), softened

2/3 cup sugar

1/4 cup skim milk

2 tablespoons all-purpose flour

2 teaspoons vanilla

3 egg whites or 1/2 cup fat-free cholesterol-free egg product

1 tablespoon baking cocoa

1 teaspoon chocolate extract

Raspberry Topping (right)

Heat oven to 300°. Spray springform pan, 9 × 3 inches, with nonstick cooking spray. Sprinkle chocolate wafer crumbs on bottom of pan. Beat Thick Yogurt and cream cheese in medium bowl with electric mixer on medium speed until smooth. Add sugar, milk, flour, vanilla and egg whites. Beat on medium speed about 2 minutes or until smooth.

Place 1 cup batter in small bowl. Beat in cocoa and chocolate extract until blended. Carefully spread vanilla batter over crumbs in pan. Drop chocolate batter by spoonfuls onto vanilla batter. Swirl through batter with metal spatula for marbled design, being careful not to touch bottom.

Bake 1 hour. Turn off oven; leave cheesecake in oven with door closed 30 minutes. Cool 15 minutes. Prepare Raspberry Topping; spread over cheesecake. Cover and refrigerate at least 3 hours.

RASPBERRY TOPPING

1 package (10 ounces) frozen raspberries, thawed, drained and juice reserved

1/4 cup sugar

1 tablespoon plus 1 1/2 teaspoons cornstarch

Add enough water to reserved raspberry juice to measure 1 1/4 cups. Mix sugar and cornstarch in 1 1/2-quart saucepan. Stir in juice mixture and raspberries. Heat to boiling over medium heat, stirring frequently. Boil and stir 1 minute. Cool; strain if desired.

1 Serving:		% Daily Value:	
Calories	195	Vitamin A	4%
Calories from fat	45	Vitamin C	2%
Fat, g	5	Calcium	14%
Saturated, g	3	Iron	2%
Cholesterol, mg	15	**Diet Exchanges:**	
Sodium, mg	150	Starch/Bread	1 1/2
Carbohydrate, g	31	Skim milk	1/2
Dietary Fiber, g	1	Fat	1
Protein, g	7		

Chocolate-Orange Angel Food Cake

16 SERVINGS

⊠ � ♥

1 1/2 cups powdered sugar

3/4 cup cake flour

1/4 cup baking cocoa

1 1/2 cups egg whites (about 12)

1 1/2 teaspoons cream of tartar

1 cup granulated sugar

1/4 teaspoon salt

3 cups orange sherbet, softened

Chocolate Sauce (page 202), if desired

Move oven rack to lowest position. Heat oven to 375°. Sift together powdered sugar, flour and cocoa; set aside. Beat egg whites and cream of tartar in large bowl with electric mixer on medium speed until foamy. Beat in granulated sugar, 2 tablespoons at a time, on high speed, adding salt with the last addition of sugar. Continue beating until stiff and glossy. Do not underbeat.

Sprinkle cocoa mixture, 1/4 cup at a time, over meringue, folding in just until cocoa mixture disappears. Spread batter in ungreased angel food cake pan (tube pan), 10 × 4 inches. Gently cut through batter with metal spatula.

Bake 30 to 35 minutes or until cracks feel dry and top springs back when touched lightly. Invert pan onto heatproof funnel or bottle about 2 hours or until cake is completely cool. Loosen side of cake with knife or long, metal spatula; remove from pan.

Slice off top of cake about 1 inch down; set aside. Cut down into cake 1 inch from outer edge and 1 inch from edge of hole, leaving substantial "walls" on each side. Remove cake within cuts with curved knife or spoon, being careful to leave a base of cake 1 inch thick. Spoon sherbet into cake cavity; smooth top. Replace top of cake. Cover and freeze about 3 hours or until firm. Serve with Chocolate Sauce.

1 Serving:		% Daily Value:	
Calories	180	Vitamin A	0%
Calories from fat	10	Vitamin C	0%
Fat, g	1	Calcium	2%
Saturated, g	1	Iron	4%
Cholesterol, mg	2	**Diet Exchanges:**	
Sodium, mg	90	Starch/Bread	1 1/2
Carbohydrate, g	40	Fruit	1
Dietary Fiber, g	0		
Protein, g	3		

Double Chocolate–Date Cake

8 SERVINGS

Chocolate Chip Topping (right)

1 cup hot water

2/3 cup chopped dates

1 2/3 cups all-purpose flour

1 cup packed brown sugar

1/4 cup baking cocoa

1 teaspoon baking soda

1/4 teaspoon salt

1/4 cup vegetable oil

1 teaspoon cider vinegar

1/2 teaspoon vanilla

Heat oven to 350°. Prepare Chocolate Chip Topping. Pour hot water over dates in small bowl. Let stand 5 minutes. Drain dates, reserving water.

Mix flour, brown sugar, cocoa, baking soda and salt in ungreased square pan, 8 × 8 × 2 inches. Stir in dates. Add enough water to date water to measure 1 cup. Stir water mixture and remaining ingredients into flour mixture. Sprinkle with topping. Bake 35 to 40 minutes or until toothpick inserted in center comes out clean.

CHOCOLATE CHIP TOPPING

2 tablespoons miniature semisweet chocolate chips

2 tablespoons chopped walnuts

2 tablespoons packed brown sugar

Mix all ingredients.

1 Serving:		% Daily Value:	
Calories	345	Vitamin A	0%
Calories from fat	80	Vitamin C	0%
Fat, g	9	Calcium	4%
Saturated, g	2	Iron	14%
Cholesterol, mg	0	**Diet Exchanges:**	
Sodium, mg	240	Not recommended	
Carbohydrate, g	64		
Dietary Fiber, g	2		
Protein, g	4		

Lemon Meringue Cake with Strawberries

9 SERVINGS

◐ ♥

A fat-free frosting? You bet! A meringue frosting makes this cake special and heart friendly.

2 cups sliced strawberries

1/4 cup sugar

1 1/4 cups all-purpose flour

1 cup sugar

1/4 cup margarine or spread, softened

1/2 cup skim milk

1 1/2 teaspoons baking powder

1 1/2 teaspoons grated lemon peel

1 teaspoon vanilla

1/4 teaspoon salt

2 egg whites or 1/4 cup fat-free cholesterol-free egg product

2 egg whites

1/2 cup sugar

Mix strawberries and 1/4 cup sugar. Cover and refrigerate until serving time.

Heat oven to 350°. Spray square pan, 9 × 9 × 2 inches, with nonstick cooking spray. Beat flour, 1 cup sugar, the margarine, milk, baking powder, lemon peel, vanilla, salt and 2 egg whites in large bowl with electric mixer on low speed 30 seconds, scraping bowl constantly. Beat on high speed 2 minutes, scraping bowl occasionally. Pour into pan. Bake 25 to 30 minutes or until toothpick inserted in center comes out clean.

Increase oven temperature to 400°. Beat 2 egg whites in medium bowl until foamy. Beat in 1/2 cup sugar, 1 tablespoon at a time. Continue beating until stiff and glossy. Spread over cake. Bake 8 to 10 minutes or until meringue is light brown. Cool completely. Top each serving with strawberries.

1 Serving:		% Daily Value:	
Calories	280	Vitamin A	8%
Calories from fat	45	Vitamin C	16%
Fat, g	5	Calcium	6%
Saturated, g	1	Iron	6%
Cholesterol, mg	0	**Diet Exchanges:**	
Sodium, mg	230	Starch/Bread	2 1/2
Carbohydrate, g	56	Fruit	1
Dietary Fiber, g	1	Fat	1
Protein, g	4		

Lemon Meringue Cake with Strawberries

Lemon-Ginger Trifle with Apricots

8 SERVINGS (ABOUT 1 CUP EACH)

◆ ♥

Angel food cakes that are either store-bought or home-made, from scratch or a mix, all work well in this recipe. A 7-inch loaf yields about 6 cups of cake cubes, and a 7 1/2-inch ring yields about 11 cups.

3/4 cup sugar

2 tablespoons cornstarch

1/4 teaspoon salt

1 1/4 cups water

1 teaspoon grated lemon peel

1/4 cup lemon juice

2 teaspoons margarine or spread

**1 1/2 teaspoons grated gingerroot
    or 1/2 teaspoon ground ginger**

**1/2 package (2.8-ounce size) whipped
    topping mix (1 envelope)**

8 cups 1-inch cubes angel food cake

6 large apricots, thinly sliced*

Mix sugar, cornstarch and salt in 2-quart saucepan. Gradually stir in water. Cook over medium heat, stirring constantly, until mixture thickens and boils. Boil and stir 1 minute; remove from heat. Stir in lemon peel, lemon juice, margarine and gingerroot. Press plastic wrap or waxed paper onto surface. Refrigerate about 4 hours or until chilled.

Prepare whipped topping mix as directed on package—except use skim milk. Reserve 3/4 cup whipped topping. Fold lemon mixture into remaining whipped topping.

Place one-third of the cake cubes in large clear glass bowl. Spread one-third of the lemon mixture over cake cubes. Top with one-third of the apricots. Repeat twice. Spread reserved whipped topping over top. Garnish with lemon curls if desired. Cover and refrigerate up to 8 hours.

*1 can (16 ounces) apricot halves in juice, well drained and sliced, can be substituted for the fresh apricots.

1 Serving:		% Daily Value:	
Calories	260	Vitamin A	4%
Calories from fat	20	Vitamin C	8%
Fat, g	2	Calcium	0%
Saturated, g	1	Iron	4%
Cholesterol, mg	0	**Diet Exchanges:**	
Sodium, mg	160	Starch/Bread	2
Carbohydrate, g	57	Fruit	2
Dietary Fiber, g	1		
Protein, g	4		

Low-Fat Thirst Quenchers

Fruit-based or dairy-based, the coolers that follow will hit the spot without causing you to hit the quilt. Bottoms up!

PEACH YOGURT COOLER

2 SERVINGS

1 can (8 ounces) sliced peaches in juice, drained

1/2 cup skim milk

1 container (6 ounces) peach low-fat yogurt (2/3 cup)

Place all ingredients in blender. Cover and blend on high speed about 30 seconds or until smooth. Pour into 2 glasses.

1 Serving:		% Daily Value:	
Calories	130	Vitamin A	6%
Calories from fat	10	Vitamin C	8%
Fat, g	1	Calcium	20%
Saturated, g	1	Iron	0%
Cholesterol, mg	5	**Diet Exchanges:**	
Sodium, mg	80	Fruit	1
Carbohydrate, g	25	Skim milk	1/2
Dietary Fiber, g	1		
Protein, g	6		

ORANGE SLUSH

8 SERVINGS

1/2 gallon vanilla fat-free frozen yogurt

1 cup frozen (thawed) orange juice concentrate

1/2 cup skim milk

Place half of the yogurt, half of the juice concentrate and half of the milk in blender. Cover and blend on medium speed about 45 seconds, stopping blender occasionally to scrape sides, until thick and smooth. Pour into 4 glasses. Repeat with remaining yogurt, juice concentrate and milk.

1 Serving:		% Daily Value:	
Calories	265	Vitamin A	10%
Calories from fat	0	Vitamin C	90%
Fat, g	0	Calcium	20%
Saturated, g	0	Iron	0%
Cholesterol, mg	2	**Diet Exchanges:**	
Sodium, mg	110	Fruit	3
Carbohydrate, g	60	Skim milk	1
Dietary Fiber, g	0		
Protein, g	6		

(Continued on next page)

Foamy Refresher

4 SERVINGS

1/4 cup iced tea mix (dry)

2 cans (12 ounces each) grapefruit soda pop, chilled

1 pint lemon fat-free frozen yogurt

Place 1 tablespoon of the tea mix in each of 4 large glasses. Add soda pop. Stir until tea mix is dissolved. Scoop sherbet into each glass.

1 Serving:		% Daily Value:	
Calories	195	Vitamin A	4%
Calories from fat	0	Vitamin C	4%
Fat, g	0	Calcium	10%
Saturated, g	0	Iron	0%
Cholesterol, mg	0	**Diet Exchanges:**	
Sodium, mg	75	Fruit	3
Carbohydrate, g	47		
Dietary Fiber, g	0		
Protein, g	2		

Tropical Tea

6 SERVINGS

2 1/4 cups water

2 cups iced tea

1/2 can (12-ounce size) frozen pineapple-orange-guava juice concentrate, thawed

Fresh mint, if desired

Mix water, iced tea and juice concentrate. Serve over ice. Garnish with mint.

1 Serving:		% Daily Value:	
Calories	45	Vitamin A	0%
Calories from fat	0	Vitamin C	34%
Fat, g	0	Calcium	0%
Saturated, g	0	Iron	0%
Cholesterol, mg	0	**Diet Exchanges:**	
Sodium, mg	3	Fruit	1
Carbohydrate, g	11		
Dietary Fiber, g	0		
Protein, g	0		

MINTY LEMONADE FREEZE

8 SERVINGS

1 large bunch mint (about 10 sprigs)

1/2 cup sugar

1 cup lemon juice (about 5 lemons)

1/2 cup water

1 bottle (1 liter) ginger ale, chilled

Crushed ice

1 Serving:		% Daily Value:	
Calories	85	Vitamin A	0%
Calories from fat	0	Vitamin C	12%
Fat, g	0	Calcium	0%
Saturated, g	0	Iron	0%
Cholesterol, mg	0	**Diet Exchanges:**	
Sodium, mg	15	Fruit	1 1/2
Carbohydrate, g	21		
Dietary Fiber, g	0		
Protein, g	0		

Wash mint; remove leaves from stems. Place leaves in pitcher. Sprinkle sugar over mint leaves. Add lemon juice and water. Let stand 30 minutes. Add ginger ale and ice. Stir vigorously until pitcher becomes frosted.

STRAWBERRY SPRITZER

8 SERVINGS

3 cups strawberries or 1 package
(16 ounces) frozen unsweetened
strawberries, partially thawed

1/4 cup orange-flavored liqueur
or orange juice

1 bottle (750 milliliters) dry white
wine, chilled

1 bottle (1 liter) mineral water or
sparkling water, chilled

Pour about 3 tablespoons strawberry mixture over ice in each of 8 tall glasses. Stir about 1/3 cup wine and 1/2 cup mineral water into each glass. Garnish side of glass with whole strawberry if desired.

1 Serving:		% Daily Value:	
Calories	60	Vitamin A	0%
Calories from fat	0	Vitamin C	52%
Fat, g	0	Calcium	0%
Saturated, g	0	Iron	2%
Cholesterol, mg	0	**Diet Exchanges:**	
Sodium, mg	5	Fruit	1/2
Carbohydrate, g	7		
Dietary Fiber, g	1		
Protein, g	0		

Place strawberries and liqueur in blender. Cover and blend on high speed about 30 seconds or until smooth.

Blueberry-Lime Torte

8 ERVINGS

⧗ ◊ ♡

Meringue Shell (right)

2 egg whites

1 egg

1/2 cup sugar

2/3 cup water

1/3 cup lime juice

1 envelope unflavored gelatin

1 tablespoon grated lime peel

1 container (8 ounces) frozen reduced-fat whipped topping, thawed

1 1/2 cups blueberries

Bake Meringue Shell; cool completely. Beat 2 egg whites and the egg in medium bowl until foamy. Mix sugar, water, lime juice and gelatin in 2-quart nonstick saucepan. Heat to boiling over medium heat, stirring constantly.

Gradually stir at least half of the hot mixture into egg mixture; stir back into hot mixture in saucepan. Heat to boiling; remove from heat. Stir in lime peel. Place pan in bowl of ice and water, or refrigerate about 15 minutes, stirring occasionally, until mixture mounds when dropped from spoon.

Fold whipped topping into lime mixture. Place blueberries in shell. Spoon lime mixture over blueberries. Refrigerate about 3 hours or until set. Garnish with lime twist and blueberries if desired.

MERINGUE SHELL

3 egg whites

1/4 teaspoon cream of tartar

3/4 cup sugar

Heat oven to 275°. Line cookie sheet with cooking parchment paper or aluminum foil. Beat egg whites and cream of tartar in medium bowl until foamy. Beat in sugar, 1 tablespoon at a time. Continue beating until stiff and glossy. Do not underbeat. Shape meringue on cookie sheet into 9-inch circle with back of spoon, building up side. Bake 1 hour. Turn off oven; leave meringue in oven with door closed 1 1/2 hours. Finish cooling meringue at room temperature.

1 Serving:		% Daily Value:	
Calories	230	Vitamin A	2%
Calories from fat	35	Vitamin C	10%
Fat, g	4	Calcium	2%
Saturated, g	3	Iron	0%
Cholesterol, mg	25	**Diet Exchanges:**	
Sodium, mg	70	Starch/Bread	1
Carbohydrate, g	43	Fruit	2
Dietary Fiber, g	0	Fat	1
Protein, g	5		

Easy Pumpkin-Orange Pie

8 SERVINGS

Love pies but don't want all of those fat calories in the crust? The solution is so simple—just get rid of it.

Brown Sugar Topping (right)

1 can (16 ounces) pumpkin

1 can (12 ounces) evaporated skimmed milk

3 egg whites or 1/2 cup fat-free cholesterol-free egg product

1/2 cup sugar

1/2 cup all-purpose flour

1 1/2 teaspoons pumpkin pie spice

3/4 teaspoon baking powder

1/8 teaspoon salt

2 teaspoons grated orange peel

Heat oven to 350°. Spray pie plate, 10 × 1 1/2 inches, with nonstick cooking spray. Prepare Brown Sugar Topping. Place remaining ingredients in blender or food processor in order listed. Cover and blend until smooth. Pour into pie plate. Sprinkle with topping.

Bake 50 to 55 minutes or until knife inserted in center comes out clean. Cool 15 minutes. Refrigerate about 4 hours or until chilled.

BROWN SUGAR TOPPING

1/4 cup packed brown sugar

1/4 cup quick-cooking oats

1 tablespoon margarine or spread, softened

Mix all ingredients.

1 Serving:		% Daily Value:	
Calories	185	Vitamin A	100%
Calories from fat	20	Vitamin C	2%
Fat, g	2	Calcium	18%
Saturated, g	0	Iron	8%
Cholesterol, mg	2	**Diet Exchanges:**	
Sodium, mg	170	Starch/Bread	2 1/2
Carbohydrate, g	37		
Dietary Fiber, g	1		
Protein, g	6		

Apple-Cranberry Crisp

6 SERVINGS (ABOUT 2/3 CUP EACH)

Reduced-fat sour cream replaces some of the margarine in the "crisp" topping in our version of the ever-versatile apple crisp.

**5 cups sliced peeled tart apples
(6 medium apples)**

1/2 cup cranberries

1/4 cup raisins

1/4 cup packed brown sugar

1/2 cup all-purpose flour

1/2 cup packed brown sugar

1/4 cup old-fashioned oats

1/2 teaspoon ground cinnamon

2 tablespoons reduced-fat sour cream

2 tablespoons firm margarine or spread

Heat oven to 350°. Spray rectangular pan, 13 × 9 × 2 inches, with nonstick cooking spray. Mix apples, cranberries, raisins and 1/4 cup brown sugar. Spread evenly in pan.

Mix flour, 1/2 cup brown sugar, the oats and cinnamon in medium bowl. Cut in sour cream and margarine, using pastry blender or crisscrossing 2 knives, until mixture is crumbly. Sprinkle over fruit. Bake about 50 minutes or until brown and bubbly.

1 Serving:		% Daily Value:	
Calories	295	Vitamin A	8%
Calories from fat	45	Vitamin C	4%
Fat, g	5	Calcium	4%
Saturated, g	1	Iron	8%
Cholesterol, mg	5	**Diet Exchanges:**	
Sodium, mg	65	Starch/Bread	1
Carbohydrate, g	64	Fruit	3
Dietary Fiber, g	3	Fat	1
Protein, g	3		

Apple-Cranberry Crisp, Grilled Peaches with Blackberry Sauce (page 184)

Orange and Currant Bread Pudding

8 SERVINGS (1/2 CUP PUDDING AND 2 TABLESPOONS SAUCE EACH)

2 tablespoons orange-flavored liqueur or orange juice

1/2 cup currants

3 cups skim milk

1 container (8 ounces) fat-free cholesterol-free egg product (1 cup)

1 teaspoon vanilla

2/3 cup packed brown sugar

2 tablespoons grated orange peel

1/2 loaf (1-pound size) French bread, cubed

Ground cinnamon

Maple-Orange Sauce (right)

Pour liqueur over currants in small bowl. Let stand 10 minutes.

Heat oven to 325°. Spray square pan, 8 × 8 × 2 inches, with nonstick cooking spray. Mix milk, egg product, vanilla, brown sugar and orange peel in large bowl. Stir in bread cubes and currant mixture. Pour into pan. Sprinkle with cinnamon. Bake 35 to 45 minutes or until light brown and center is set. Serve warm or cool with Maple-Orange Sauce.

MAPLE-ORANGE SAUCE

1 teaspoon cornstarch

1 cup orange juice

3 tablespoons maple-flavored syrup

Mix all ingredients in 1-quart saucepan. Cook over medium-high heat 3 to 5 minutes, stirring constantly, until sauce thickens. Serve warm.

1 Serving:		% Daily Value:	
Calories	220	Vitamin A	6%
Calories from fat	10	Vitamin C	12%
Fat, g	1	Calcium	16%
Saturated, g	0	Iron	10%
Cholesterol, mg	2	**Diet Exchanges:**	
Sodium, mg	180	Starch/Bread	2
Carbohydrate, g	47	Fruit	1
Dietary Fiber, g	1		
Protein, g	7		

Creamy Peach Freeze

8 SERVINGS (ABOUT 1/2 CUP EACH)

1/2 cup fat-free cholesterol-free egg product

2/3 cup sugar

1 1/2 cups skim milk

1/4 teaspoon salt

**2 cups mashed peeled peaches
(4 to 5 medium)***

2 teaspoons vanilla

**2 containers (8 ounces each) peach fat-free
yogurt**

Mix egg product, sugar, milk and salt in 2-quart saucepan. Cook over medium heat, stirring constantly, just until bubbles appear around edge. Pour into chilled large metal bowl. Refrigerate 1 1/2 to 2 hours, stirring occasionally, until room temperature.

Stir peaches, vanilla and yogurt into milk mixture. Pour into 1-quart ice-cream freezer and freeze according to manufacturer's directions.

*1 package (16 ounces) frozen sliced peaches, thawed and mashed, can be substituted for the fresh peaches.

1 Serving:		% Daily Value:	
Calories	140	Vitamin A	10%
Calories from fat	0	Vitamin C	6%
Fat, g	0	Calcium	14%
Saturated, g	0	Iron	4%
Cholesterol, mg	2	**Diet Exchanges:**	
Sodium, mg	135	Fruit	2
Carbohydrate, g	31		
Dietary Fiber, g	1		
Protein, g	5		

Three-Berry Sorbet

4 SERVINGS (1 CUP EACH)

Sorbet is French for sherbet. Unlike sherbets, however, sorbets do not contain milk or cream, making them the perfect fat-free frozen dessert.

1 1/2 cups frozen unsweetened raspberries, partially thawed

1 1/2 cups frozen unsweetened blackberries, partially thawed

1 1/2 cups frozen unsweetened blueberries, partially thawed

1/2 cup orange juice

1/4 cup maple-flavored syrup, sugar, honey or packed brown sugar

2 tablespoons frozen (thawed) apple juice concentrate

1/4 teaspoon vanilla

Place all ingredients in blender or food processor. Cover and blend on medium-high speed, stopping occasionally to scrape sides, until very smooth. Pour into 1-quart ice-cream freezer and freeze according to manufacturer's directions.

Or, pour into loaf pan, 9 × 5 × 3 inches. Cover and freeze about 2 hours or until edges are firm but center is soft. Spoon partially frozen mixture into blender or food processor. Cover and blend on medium-high speed until smooth. Pour into pan. Cover and freeze about 3 hours or until firm. Let stand 10 minutes at room temperature before spooning into dessert dishes.

1 Serving:		% Daily Value:	
Calories	195	Vitamin A	2%
Calories from fat	10	Vitamin C	96%
Fat, g	1	Calcium	6%
Saturated, g	0	Iron	8%
Cholesterol, mg	0	**Diet Exchanges:**	
Sodium, mg	10	Fruit	3
Carbohydrate, g	50		
Dietary Fiber, g	5		
Protein, g	2		

Three-Berry Sorbet, Biscotti (page 204)

Chocolate Sauce

ABOUT **1 3/4** CUPS SAUCE

You'll want to make sure you keep a supply of this versatile sauce on hand whether it be for topping fat-free frozen yogurt or fresh fruit or stirring into skim milk for quick chocolate milk.

1/2 cup sugar

1/4 cup baking cocoa

1 tablespoon cornstarch

1 can (12 ounces) evaporated skimmed milk

1 teaspoon vanilla

Mix sugar, cocoa and cornstarch in 1 1/2-quart saucepan. Gradually stir in milk. Heat over medium heat, stirring constantly, until mixture thickens and boils; remove from heat. Stir in vanilla. (Beat with wire whisk if sauce becomes lumpy.) Serve warm, or press plastic wrap or waxed paper onto surface and refrigerate until chilled.

1 Tablespoon:		% Daily Value:	
Calories	30	Vitamin A	0%
Calories from fat	0	Vitamin C	0%
Fat, g	0	Calcium	4%
Saturated, g	0	Iron	0%
Cholesterol, mg	0	**Diet Exchanges:**	
Sodium, mg	15	Starch/Bread	1/2
Carbohydrate, g	6		
Dietary Fiber, g	0		
Protein, g	1		

Peppermint Brownies

16 BROWNIES

Don't like peppermint? No problem; leave out the peppermint extract and you have traditional brownies—without the extra fat.

1 cup sugar

1/3 cup margarine or spread, softened

1 teaspoon vanilla

1/2 teaspoon peppermint extract

3 egg whites or 1/2 cup fat-free cholesterol-free egg product

2/3 cup all-purpose flour

1/2 cup baking cocoa

1/2 teaspoon baking powder

1/4 teaspoon salt

Chocolate Glaze (right)

2 tablespoons crushed peppermint candy

Heat oven to 350°. Spray square pan, 8 × 8 × 2 inches, with nonstick cooking spray. Mix sugar, margarine, vanilla, peppermint extract and egg whites in medium bowl. Stir in flour, cocoa, baking powder and salt. Spread in pan.

Bake 20 to 25 minutes or until toothpick inserted in center comes out clean; cool. Spread Chocolate Glaze evenly over brownies. Sprinkle with candy. Cut into about 2-inch squares.

Chocolate Glaze

2/3 cup powdered sugar

2 tablespoons baking cocoa

1/4 teaspoon vanilla

3 to 4 teaspoons hot water

Mix all ingredients until smooth and spreadable.

1 Brownie:		% Daily Value:	
Calories	140	Vitamin A	4%
Calories from fat	35	Vitamin C	0%
Fat, g	4	Calcium	2%
Saturated, g	1	Iron	4%
Cholesterol, mg	0	Diet Exchanges:	
Sodium, mg	105	Starch/Bread	1
Carbohydrate, g	25	Fruit	1
Dietary Fiber, g	1		
Protein, g	2		

Frosted Banana Bars

24 BARS

2/3 cup sugar

1/2 cup reduced-fat sour cream

2 tablespoons margarine or spread, softened

2 egg whites or 1/4 cup fat-free
   cholesterol-free egg product

3/4 cup mashed very ripe bananas
   (about 2 medium)

1 teaspoon vanilla

1 cup all-purpose flour

1/4 teaspoon salt

1/2 teaspoon baking soda

2 tablespoons finely chopped walnuts

Frosting (right)

Heat oven to 375°. Spray square pan, $9 \times 9 \times 2$ inches, with nonstick cooking spray. Beat sugar, sour cream, margarine and egg whites in large bowl with electric mixer on low speed 1 minute, scraping bowl occasionally. Beat in bananas and vanilla on low speed 30 seconds. Beat in flour, salt and baking soda on medium speed 1 minute, scraping bowl occasionally. Stir in nuts. Spread in pan.

Bake 20 to 25 minutes or until light brown. Cool completely. Spread with Frosting. Cut into $2 1/4 \times 1 1/2$-inch bars.

Frosting

1 1/4 cups powdered sugar

1 tablespoon margarine or spread, softened

1/2 teaspoon vanilla

1 to 2 tablespoons skim milk

Mix all ingredients until smooth and spreadable.

1 Bar:		% Daily Value:	
Calories	100	Vitamin A	2%
Calories from fat	20	Vitamin C	0%
Fat, g	2	Calcium	0%
Saturated, g	1	Iron	2%
Cholesterol, mg	2	Diet Exchanges:	
Sodium, mg	75	Starch/Bread	1
Carbohydrate, g	19		
Dietary Fiber, g	0		
Protein, g	1		

Chocolate Chip Cookies

ABOUT 2 1/2 DOZEN COOKIES

This cookie has half the fat and half the chips of ordinary chocolate chip cookies, but you won't miss them. Miniature chips give the illusion of more chocolate because they distribute so well.

1/2 cup granulated sugar

1/4 cup packed brown sugar

1/4 cup margarine or spread, softened

1 teaspoon vanilla

1 egg white or 2 tablespoons fat-free cholesterol-free egg product

1 cup all-purpose flour

1/2 teaspoon baking soda

1/4 teaspoon salt

1/2 cup miniature semisweet chocolate chips

Heat oven to 375°. Mix sugars, margarine, vanilla and egg white in large bowl. Stir in flour, baking soda and salt. Stir in chocolate chips.

Drop dough by rounded teaspoonfuls about 2 inches apart onto ungreased cookie sheet. Bake 8 to 10 minutes or until golden brown. Cool slightly; remove from cookie sheet. Cool on wire rack.

1 Cookie:		% Daily Value:	
Calories	60	Vitamin A	2%
Calories from fat	20	Vitamin C	0%
Fat, g	2	Calcium	0%
Saturated, g	1	Iron	2%
Cholesterol, mg	0	**Diet Exchanges:**	
Sodium, mg	60	Fruit	1
Carbohydrate, g	10		
Dietary Fiber, g	0		
Protein, g	1		

Biscotti

ABOUT 4 DOZEN BISCOTTI

1 cup sugar

1/2 cup margarine or spread, softened

5 egg whites or 3/4 cup fat-free cholesterol-free egg product

1 1/4 teaspoons almond extract

3 1/2 cups all-purpose flour

1 teaspoon baking powder

1/2 teaspoon salt

2 cups ground almonds (8 ounces)

Heat oven to 350°. Grease rectangular pan, 13 × 9 × 2 inches. Beat sugar and margarine in large bowl with electric mixer on medium speed until creamy. Beat in egg whites and almond extract on high speed about 2 minutes or until light and fluffy. Stir in flour, baking powder and salt. Stir in almonds. Spread in pan. Bake 25 to 30 minutes or until toothpick inserted in center comes out clean. Cool completely.

Heat oven to 350°. Cut cake crosswise into four 3-inch strips. Cut strips diagonally or crosswise into 1/2-inch slices. Place on ungreased cookie sheet. Bake 20 to 25 minutes or until crisp and brown. Remove from cookie sheet. Cool on wire rack.

1 Biscotti:		% Daily Value:	
Calories	90	Vitamin A	2%
Calories from fat	35	Vitamin C	0%
Fat, g	4	Calcium	2%
Saturated, g	1	Iron	2%
Cholesterol, mg	0	**Diet Exchanges:**	
Sodium, mg	60	Starch/Bread	1
Carbohydrate, g	12		
Dietary Fiber, g	1		
Protein, g	2		

Chocolate Chip Cookies, Cocoa-Oatmeal Cookies (page 206)

Cocoa-Oatmeal Cookies

ABOUT 5 1/2 DOZEN COOKIES

The dough may seem too liquid at first, but the oats and cocoa will absorb the excess moisture.

1 1/2 cups sugar

1/2 cup margarine or spread, softened

1/2 cup plain fat-free yogurt

1/4 cup water

1 teaspoon vanilla

1/2 teaspoon chocolate extract, if desired

2 egg whites or 1/4 cup fat-free
   cholesterol-free egg product

3 cups quick-cooking oats

1 1/4 cups all-purpose flour

1/3 cup baking cocoa

1/2 teaspoon baking soda

1/4 teaspoon salt

1/2 cup miniature semisweet chocolate
   chips*

Heat oven to 350°. Mix sugar, margarine, yogurt, water, vanilla, chocolate extract and egg whites in large bowl. Stir in remaining ingredients.

Drop dough by rounded teaspoonfuls about 2 inches apart onto ungreased cookie sheet. Bake 9 to 11 minutes or until almost no indentation remains when touched. Remove from cookie sheet. Cool on wire rack.

*1/2 cup carob chips can be substituted for the chocolate chips.

1 Cookie:		% Daily Value:	
Calories	60	Vitamin A	2%
Calories from fat	20	Vitamin C	0%
Fat, g	2	Calcium	0%
Saturated, g	1	Iron	2%
Cholesterol, mg	0	**Diet Exchanges:**	
Sodium, mg	35	Fruit	1
Carbohydrate, g	10		
Dietary Fiber, g	0		
Protein, g	1		

Appendices

Making Good Food Choices

- The Food Guide Pyramid is divided into six parts, or food groups. The top section is Fats, Oils and Sweets, and most people need to limit their use of these foods. The 5 lower groups are all important, and you need food from all of them.

- Below the name of each food group are some numbers that tell you how many servings to eat from that group each day. You need more foods from the groups at the bottom, where it is wider, than you do from the top groups.

- At each meal, serve foods from at least 3 different food groups. Some foods, such as tacos, combine foods from 2 or more different groups. Do the best you can to estimate the servings from each food group.

- It's a good idea to plan for snacks just as you plan for meals. Keep a supply of healthy snack foods on hand, such as cut-up vegetables or low-fat crackers and cookies.

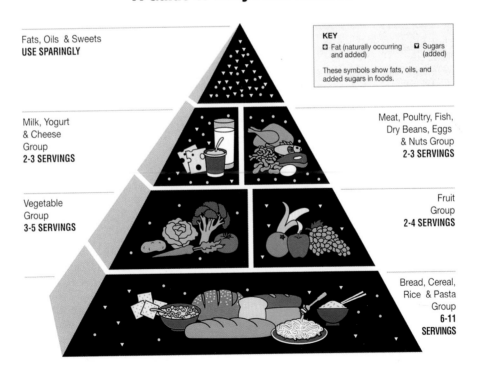

Food Guide Pyramid
A Guide to Daily Food Choices

Fats, Oils & Sweets
USE SPARINGLY

KEY
☐ Fat (naturally occurring and added)   ▾ Sugars (added)

These symbols show fats, oils, and added sugars in foods.

Milk, Yogurt & Cheese Group
2-3 SERVINGS

Meat, Poultry, Fish, Dry Beans, Eggs & Nuts Group
2-3 SERVINGS

Vegetable Group
3-5 SERVINGS

Fruit Group
2-4 SERVINGS

Bread, Cereal, Rice & Pasta Group
6-11 SERVINGS

Reading a Nutrition Label

The Nutrition Facts Label can be found on food packages in your supermarket. Reading the label tells you more about the food and the nutrients it supplies. The nutrition and ingredient information you see on the food label is required by the government.

Some food packages have a short or abbreviated nutrition label. These foods contain only a few of the nutrients required on the standard label and can use a short label format. What's on the label depends on what's in the food. Small- and medium-sized packages with very little label space also may use a short label format. Here's what the label looks like with an explanation of its new features.

Nutrition Facts Title

The new title "Nutrition Facts" signals the new label.

Serving Size

Serving sizes are standardized based on amounts people actually eat. Now similar food products have similar serving sizes making it easier to compare foods in the same category.

New Label Information

Some label information may not be familiar to you. The nutrient list covers those nutrients most important to your health. You may have seen this information on some old labels, but now it is required by the government and must appear on all food labels.

Vitamins and Minerals

The Percent Daily Value replaces the Percent U.S. RDA for vitamins and minerals. The levels are the same. Only vitamin A, vitamin C, calcium, iron, and fortified nutrients are required on the new label: additional vitamins and minerals can be listed voluntarily.

Label Numbers

Numbers on the nutrition label may be rounded for labeling.

Nutrition Facts

Serving Size 1 cup (30g)
Servings Per Container About 10

Amount Per Serving

Calories 110   Calories from Fat 10

	% Daily Value*
Total Fat 1g	**2%**
Saturated Fat 0g	**0%**
Cholesterol 0mg	**0%**
Sodium 240mg	**10%**
Total Carbohydrate 24g	**8%**
Dietary Fiber 3g	**10%**
Sugars 6g	
Protein 3g	

Vitamin A 25%	*	Vitamin C 25%
Calcium 4%	*	Iron 45%

* Percent Daily Values are based on a 2,000 calorie diet. Your daily values may be higher or lower depending on your calorie needs:

		Calories:	2,000	2,500
Total Fat	Less than		65g	80g
Sat. Fat	Less than		20g	25g
Cholesterol	Less than		300mg	300mg
Sodium	Less than		2,400mg	2,400mg
Total Carbohydrates			300g	375g
Dietary Fiber			25g	30g

Calories per gram:
Fat 0   *   Carbohydrate 4   *   Protein 4

% Daily Value

The Percent Daily Value shows how a food fits into a 2,000 calorie reference diet. These levels are based on dietary recommendations for most healthy people. Percent Daily Values help you judge whether a food contains "a lot" or "a little" of key nutrients important to health.

Daily Values Footnote

Daily Values are the new label reference numbers. These numbers are set by the government and are based on current nutrition recommendations. Some labels list Daily Values for a diet of 2,000 and 2,500 calories per day. Your own nutrient needs may be less than or more than the Daily Values on the label.

Calories Per Gram Footnote

Some labels tell the appropriate number of calories in a gram of fat, carbohydrate, and protein. (One gram is about the weight of a regular paperclip.) This information helps you calculate the percentage of calories from these nutrients.

Calorie, Fat and Cholesterol Content of Selected Foods

Food	Unit Measure	Calories	Total Fat, g	Saturated Fat, g	Cholesterol, mg
Whole milk	1 cup	150	8	5	35
2% milk	1 cup	120	5	3	20
1% milk	1 cup	100	2.5	2	10
Skim milk	1 cup	90	0	0	4
Plain yogurt	1 cup	150	8	5	30
Low-fat plain yogurt	1 cup	150	4	2	15
Fat-free plain yogurt	1 cup	140	0	0	5
Whipped heavy cream	2 tablespoons	45	5	3	15
Prepared whipped topping mix prepared with skim milk	2 tablespoons	15	0.5	0	0
Vanilla ice cream (16% fat)	1 cup	360	24	15	90
Vanilla ice milk	1 cup	180	6	3	20
Vanilla frozen yogurt	1 cup	200	2	1	10
Fat-free vanilla frozen yogurt	1 cup	200	0	0	2
Sour cream	1 cup	450	44	28	150
Reduced-fat sour cream	1 cup	320	16	10	80
Fat-free sour cream	1 cup	160	2	2	40
Creamed cottage cheese	1 cup	220	9	6	30
Low-fat cottage cheese	1 cup	200	4	3	20
Ricotta cheese, whole milk	15 ounces	800	60	38	235
Reduced-fat ricotta cheese, part skim	15 ounces	640	36	23	140

Calorie, Fat and Cholesterol Content of Selected Foods (cont'd)

Food	Unit Measure	Calories	Total Fat, g	Saturated Fat, g	Cholesterol, mg
Fat-free ricotta cheese	15 ounces	310	2.5	2	70
Cream cheese	1 ounce	100	10	6	30
Reduced-fat cream cheese (Neufchâtel)	1 ounce	70	7	4	20
Fat-free cream cheese	1 ounce	25	0	0	0
Cheddar cheese	1 ounce	110	9	6	30
Reduced-fat cheddar cheese	1 ounce	80	5	3	15
Fat-free cheddar cheese	1 ounce	50	0	0	5
Swiss cheese	1 ounce	110	8	5	25
Reduced-fat Swiss Cheese	1 ounce	70	4	3	10
Fat-free Swiss cheese	1 ounce	40	0	0	5
Eggs	1 large	70	5	2	210
Fat-free, cholesterol-free egg product	1/4 cup	20	0	0	0
Italian salad dressing	1 tablespoon, bottled	70	7	1	0
Fat-free Italian salad dressing	1 tablespoon, bottled	15	0	0	0
Blue cheese salad dressing	1 tablespoon, bottled	80	8	2	2
Fat-free blue cheese salad dressing	1 tablespoon, bottled	5	0	0	2
Egg noodles	2 ounces, dry	200	2	0	50
Cholesterol-free noodles	2 ounces, dry	220	1	0	0
White layer cake with white frosting	1/12 slice	250	11	6	2
White Angel food cake, unfrosted	1/12 slice	170	0	0	0
Potato chips	1 ounce	160	10	2	0
Tortilla chips	1 ounce	130	6	1	0
Pretzels	1 ounce	110	1	0	0

Compiled by GMI from University of Minnesota Nutrition Data System, product labels and manufacturer-provided nutrition information.

Calorie, Fat and Cholesterol Content of Meat, Poultry and Seafoods

Food	Unit Measure	Calories	Fat, g	Saturated Fat, g	Cholesterol, mg
Beef boneless rib roast	3 ounces, roasted	210	13	5	70
Sirloin steak, boneless	3 ounces, broiled	150	4	1	70
Beef tenderloin	3 ounces, roasted	180	8	3	65
Beef top round steak	3 ounces, broiled	150	4	1	70
Flank steak	3 ounces, broiled	180	8	3	65
Ground beef (25% fat)	3 ounces, broiled	260	19	8	75
Extra lean ground beef (10% fat)	3 ounces, broiled	180	8	3	65
Pork tenderloin	3 ounces, roasted	140	4	1	65
Pork loin, boneless	3 ounces, roasted	180	9	3	70
Pork shoulder blade steak	3 ounces, braised	210	13	5	70
Ground pork	3 ounces, broiled	250	17	6	80
Smoked ham, boneless	3 ounces	150	8	3	50
Chicken breast, with skin	3 ounces, roasted	180	8	2	70
Chicken breast, skinless	3 ounces, roasted	140	3	1	65
Chicken thigh, with skin	3 ounces, roasted	200	12	3	75
Chicken thigh, skinless	3 ounces, roasted	170	7	2	75
Turkey, white meat without skin	3 ounces, roasted	140	3	1	65
Turkey, dark meat without skin	3 ounces, roasted	170	7	2	75
Tuna, oil-packed, drained	3 ounces, canned	170	7	1	15
Tuna, water-packed, drained	3 ounces, canned	100	1	0	25
Salmon, Chinook	3 ounces, baked	120	5	1	45
Flounder, sole	3 ounces, baked	100	1	0	60
Shrimp, without shells	3 ounces, cooked	80	1	0	165
Crab legs	3 ounces, cooked	90	2	0	85
Imitation seafood sticks	3 ounces, cooked	85	1	0	25
Scallops, without shells	3 ounces, cooked	100	1	0	25
Clams, without shells	3 ounces, cooked	130	2	0	55

Source: Compiled by GMI from University of Minnesota Nutrition Data System, product labels and manufacturer-provided nutrition information.

Fat Content of Fish

Lean Fish (less than 2.5% fat)	Medium-fat fish (2.5–5% fat)	Fatty fish (more than 5% fat)
Cod	Anchovy	Butterfish
Haddock	Bluefish	Herring
Halibut	Catfish	Mackerel: Atlantic, Pacific, Spanish
Grouper	Croaker	Pompano
Mackerel: king	Mullet	Sablefish
Mahimahi	Porgy	Salmon: Chinook, Coho, Sockeye
Ocean perch	Redfish	Sardines
Orange roughy	Salmon: pink	Shad
Pike	Shark	Tuna: albacore
Red snapper	Swordfish	Trout: lake
Sole	Trout: rainbow, sea	
Striped bass	Tuna: bluefin	
Tuna: skipjack, yellowfin	Whitefish	

Compiled by General Mills, Inc., from Fisheries Institute, 1990.

Egg White Substitutions for Whole Eggs*

Use	For	Use	For
2 egg whites	1 whole egg	8 egg whites	5 whole eggs
3 egg whites	2 whole eggs	9 egg whites	6 whole eggs
5 egg whites	3 whole eggs	11 egg whites	7 whole eggs
6 egg whites	4 whole eggs	12 egg whites	8 whole eggs

Based on whole large eggs (about 1/4 cup each).
Source: General Mills, Inc., 1990.

Calorie, Fat and Cholesterol Content of Oils and Fats

Food	Unit Measure	Calories	Total Fat, g	Saturated Fat, g	Cholesterol, mg
Lard	1 tablespoon	120	13	5	10
Solid vegetable shortening	1 tablespoon	110	13	3	0
Butter	1 tablespoon	100	12	7	30
Stick corn oil margarine	1 tablespoon	100	12	2	0
Tub vegetable oil spread (60% fat)	1 tablespoon	80	9	2	0
Tub reduced-calorie margarine	1 tablespoon	50	6	1	0
Corn oil	1 tablespoon	120	14	2	0
Olive oil	1 tablespoon	120	14	2	0
Soybean oil	1 tablespoon	120	14	2	0
Canola oil	1 tablespoon	120	14	1	0
Nonstick cooking spray	1 spray (2.5 seconds)	5	0	0	0
Mayonnaise, soybean	1 tablespoon	100	11	2	10
Cholesterol-free reduced-calorie mayonnaise	1 tablespoon	50	5	1	0
Fat-free mayonnaise	1 tablespoon	10	0	0	0

Compiled by GMI from University of Minnesota Nutrition Data System, product labels and manufacturer-provided nutrition information.

Helpful Nutrition and Cooking Information

Nutrition Guidelines:

Daily Values are set by the Food and Drug Administration and are based on the needs of most healthy adults. Percent Daily Values are based on an average diet of 2,000 calories per day. Your daily values may be higher or lower depending on your calorie needs.

Recommended intake for a daily diet of 2,000 calories:

Total Fat	Less than 65 g
Saturated Fat	Less than 20 g
Cholesterol	Less than 300 mg
Sodium	Less than 2,400 mg
Total Carbohydrate	300 g
Dietary Fiber	25 g

Criteria Used for Calculating Nutrition Information:

- The first ingredient is used wherever a choice is given (such as 1/3 cup sour cream or plain yogurt).

- The first ingredient amount is used wherever a range is given (such as 2 to 3 teaspoons milk).

- The first serving number is used wherever a range is given (such as 4 to 6 servings).

- "If desired" ingredients are not included, whether mentioned in the ingredient list or in the recipe directions as a suggestion (such as sprinkle with brown sugar if desired).

- Only the amount of a marinade of frying oil that is absorbed during preparation is calculated.

Cooking Terms Glossary:

Beat: Make smooth with a vigorous stirring motion using a spoon, wire whisk, egg beater or electric mixer.

Boil: Heat liquid until bubbles keep rising and breaking on the surface.

Chop: Cot food into small, uneven pieces; a sharp knife, food chopper or food processor may be used.

Core: Cut out the stem end and remove the seeds.

Cut in: Mix fat into a flour mixture with a pastry blender with a rolling motion or cutting with a fork or two knives until particles are size specified.

Dice: Cut into cubes smaller than 1/2 inch.

Drain: Pour off liquid or let it run off through the holes in a strainer or colander, as when draining cooked pasta or ground beef. Or, remove pieces of food from a fat or liquid and set them on paper towels to soak up excess moisture.

Flute: Flatten pastry evenly on rim of pie plate and press firmly around rim with tines of fork.

Grate: Rub against small holes of grater to cut into tiny pieces.

Grease: Spread the bottoms and side of a disk or pan with solid vegetable shortening using a pastry brush or paper towel.

Knead: Curve your fingers and fold dough toward you, then push it away with the heels of your hands, using a quick rocking motion.

Mix: combine to distribute ingredients evenly using a spoon, fork, blender or an electric mixer.

Peel: Cut off the skin with a knife or peel with fingers.

Pipe: Press out frosting from a decorating bag using steady pressure to form a design or write a message. To finish a design, stop the pressure and lift the pint up and away.

Roll or **Pat:** Flatten and spread with a floured rolling pin or hands.

Ingredients used in recipe testing and nutrition calculations:

- Large eggs, canned ready-to-use chicken broth, 2% milk, 80%-lean ground beef and vegetable-oil spread with less than 80% fat. These are used as they are the most commonly purchased ingredients within those categories.

- Regular long-grain white rice wherever cooked rice is listed, unless indicated.

- Nonfat, low-fat or low-sodium products are not used, unless indicated.

- Solid vegetable shortening (not margarine, butter and nonstick cooking sprays, as they can cause sticking problems) us used to grease pans, unless indicated.

Equipment used in Recipe Testing:

- Cookware and bakeware *without* nonstick coatings are used, unless indicated.

- Wherever a baking *pan* is specified in a recipe, a *metal* pan is used; wherever a baking *dish* or pie *plate* is specified, ovenproof *glass* or *ceramic* ovenware is used.

- A portable electric hand mixer is used for mixing *only when mixer speeds are specified* in the recipe directions.

Metric Conversion Guide

Volume

U.S. Units	Canadian Metric	Australian Metric
1/4 teaspoon	1 mL	1 ml
1/2 teaspoon	2 mL	2 ml
1 teaspoon	5 mL	5 ml
1 tablespoon	15 mL	20 ml
1/4 cup	50 mL	60 ml
1/3 cup	75 mL	80 ml
1/2 cup	125 mL	125 ml
2/3 cup	150 mL	170 ml
3/4 cup	175 mL	190 ml
1 cup	250 mL	250 ml
1 quart	1 liter	1 liter
1 1/2 quarts	1.5 liters	1.5 liters
2 quarts	2 liters	2 liters
2 1/2 quarts	2.5 liters	2.5 liters
3 quarts	3 liters	3 liters
4 quarts	4 liters	4 liters

Weight

U.S. Units	Canadian Metric	Australian Metric
1 ounce	30 grams	30 grams
2 ounces	55 grams	60 grams
3 ounces	85 grams	90 grams
4 ounces (1/4 pound)	115 grams	125 grams
8 ounces (1/2 pound)	225 grams	225 grams
16 ounces (1 pound)	455 grams	500 grams
1 pound	455 grams	1/2 kilogram

Note: The recipes in this cookbook have not been developed or tested using metric measures. When converting recipes to metric, some variations in quality may be noted.

Measurements

Inches	Centimeters
1	2.5
2	5.0
3	7.5
4	10.0
5	12.5
6	15.0
7	17.5
8	20.5
9	23.0
10	25.5
11	28.0
12	30.5
13	33.0
14	35.5
15	38.0

Temperatures

Fahrenheit	Celsius
32°	0°
212°	100°
250°	120°
275°	140°
300°	150°
325°	160°
350°	180°
375°	190°
400°	200°
425°	220°
450°	230°
475°	240°
500°	260°

Index

Numbers in *italics* refer to photos.